PART ONE – CONCEPTION

(OUT)LAW

From Teenage Mum to Legal Trailblazer

Alice Stephenson

HAWKSMOOR
PUBLISHING

First published 2023 by Hawksmoor Publishing

Woodside, Oakamoor, ST10 3AE

www.hawksmoorpublishing.com

ISBN: 9781914066382

Acknowledgements

To my daughter, Lydia, you are the beacon that guides and inspires me daily. The privilege of being your mother and witnessing your journey into the remarkable young adult you've blossomed into fills me with boundless pride. Our shared experiences have enriched both our lives immeasurably.

My dearest Pete, words fall short when it comes to expressing the magnitude of my gratitude and love for you. You've stood by my side, not merely as a husband, but as a confidante, anchor, and guiding light. Your faith in me and your love have unlocked worlds I never dreamt of. The depth of your unwavering support will forever hold a cherished place in my heart.

To the wonderful Judith Cameron, without whom this book wouldn't exist. We've known each other for over 30 years, and when you told me I should write a book and you'd help me, I felt unsure about how we'd manage it. But you took the lead, and your beautiful writing brought my story to life in a way I never imagined.

James, my gratitude to you is manifold. As a first-time author, your decision to believe in my story was a leap of faith. Your sharp insights, relentless effort, and enduring patience have been instrumental in shaping this narrative.

A heartfelt thank you to my formidable team at Stephenson Law, past and present, and to the Lawscape community and my extensive professional network. Each one of you has enveloped me in a cocoon of unwavering support, kindness, and understanding, propelling me forward even in the face of adversity.

Lastly, a nod to my own spirit. For the tenacity, grit, and unyielding drive to effect meaningful change within the legal profession, I salute you. The journey is long, but the resolve is undying. Onward we march.

1. The Beginnings of Stephenson Law

I can pinpoint the moment of germination. The time when countless random ideas swimming in my head joined together to make one tiny egg – ready to gestate, mutate and grow before hatching into Stephenson Law.

It was precisely six months before the birth of my third child.

'Good to see you, Alice, and well done.' The bespectacled man smiled as he looked up at me from his computer screen, pushed his chair back and loosened his tie a little. Despite air conditioning and tinted glass, the heat from the strong May sun still penetrated the floor-to-ceiling windows of the large corner office.

'The Bull contract was a mess, and you turned it around brilliantly.' John was the senior partner at Blinkered Brothers, where I was working as a freelance solicitor.

'Thank you,' I smiled back.

'It's not the first time you've shown how capable you are under difficult circumstances,' he continued. 'I would really love you to stick around for a bit longer.'

'Happy to talk about that!' I replied eagerly. Such praise was rare, but we both knew Blinkered had very nearly lost the valuable Bull contract before I was brought in to deal with it. Another lawyer, a guy about my age but more senior than me, had made a series of mistakes I managed to clear up. 'Once some of the pre-conditions were taken into account, it turned out to be a satisfying project,' I explained.

I'd been working as a freelancer with Blinkered for a few months and decided this was probably the right time to share my own condition. I took a deep breath before adding. 'And my news is that I'm going to have another baby.'

It wasn't just his smile that dropped away, but his whole face. His jowls almost met his shirt collar, with his eyes effectively closing on me without blinking. His thin lips pursed, and he swung his chair back to the computer screen. The meeting was evidently over.

Although John never spoke to me again, he had unwittingly given me the impetus to kick back.

I'd suffered far more humiliating put-downs during my career and survived far greater traumas in my past, but his crass attitude pushed me beyond the brink. I looked at the back of his head, where a pink bald patch was partially hidden by careful grooming.

I nodded slowly with my lips pursed. Germination had just taken place. Gestation had begun.

It was time to reveal the unspoken bias women faced throughout the industry. It was time to challenge and overcome the multitude of barriers we encountered daily. It was time for change.

Of course, I had no idea that my timing was quite so apt. Nor that shortly after my yet-to-emerge child started school, my business would have more than matured, hatched and flown the nest. I had no clue that within a few short years, Stephenson Law – with its flamingo logo, unique business model, and host of industry awards – would have a great team of lawyers and a list of clients the top law firms in the country would bite their arms off to work with.

But it all began here.

2. Childhood and Being a Teenage Mum

Mine is no story of rags to riches. I was born into a comfortably middle-class family, went to a private school and had my own pony with fun-filled weekends and holidays. Along with my younger sister, I competed at shows or spent time with a great group of friends at the local stables. We all loved riding together or simply being together and mucking out at the yard. Anyone looking in from the outside would say I enjoyed a privileged childhood.

If I ever considered what I'd do as a grown-up, other than becoming a wife and mother, I would probably have said that I'd work with animals. (And I do still love animals!) As a little girl, I didn't question the role of women, either within my family or the wider community. I didn't ask why men made the big decisions, were treated as more important, or expected to be obeyed. At home, Dad was simply the boss, with Mum there to support him and look after us.

'Eat up, girls.'

On a weekday, Mum would bustle around the kitchen getting our father's evening meal ready while we were dawdling over our own. 'I want you ready for bed by the time Daddy gets home.'

'Can I show him my project on Henry Vlll and his six wives?' We didn't see much of our dad unless away on holiday, and I was eager to please.

'No, I don't think so.'

Mum talked as she cleared our plates and wiped the table before returning to her cooking. 'Daddy's very busy making big decisions all day and needs a break when he gets home. He won't want to hear your stories about any number of Henrys or their wives.'

'Can I show you, then?' Didn't Mum realise that Henry Vlll was a king who had six wives?

'Not today, Alice.'

Her reply was gentle but firm. 'Now run along with your sister and get your teeth brushed. I'll be up in a minute.'

Once we were bathed and in our pyjamas, my sister and I would watch cartoons until Dad came in from work. Sometimes, we'd even sit side by side in his big armchair and press a magic button that lifted our legs up so we'd be almost lying down in front of the TV.

'Now, now,' Mum would chastise as she came to fetch us and turn the TV off. 'You know that's Daddy's special chair and not for little girls.'

We'd jump up and duly follow Mum to give Dad a perfunctory kiss before heading off to bed. Like my sister, I was a well-behaved child and did as I was told without question.

Things changed soon after I started secondary school when I began to develop my own identity. I wanted my ideas and individuality to be recognised rather than stifled. The atmosphere of the all-girls school I attended seemed oppressive, and as the years went by, I started to push back on authority. Diversity of opinion or an exploration of ideas weren't encouraged. Instead, we were being thoroughly and effectively educated to pass public examinations. While this more than satisfied my parents' expectations, I wanted and needed more from my learning environment.

I did have a couple of good friends but generally found few girls who shared my opinions. We were encouraged to aim for careers predominantly in occupations perceived as suitable for women, such as education and medicine. Jobs that could fit around the demands of a family – teachers had long school holidays, and GPs could easily work part-time. We weren't being inspired or prepared to become future heads of industry or founders of our own companies. There was no suggestion that intelligent women should have the same opportunities as intelligent men. I refused to accept this mindset.

My strength of purpose was much more than typical teenage angst or resentment over the school's strict uniform code – I just didn't feel I fitted in anywhere. This was increasingly difficult as time went by, and caused friction and challenges at home. I became more stubborn, which caused more conflict with my parents, who were quite conservative and very different in how they saw the world. I felt I was being held back and restricted in my ability to express myself. By the time I reached my middle teens, we didn't see eye to eye on many things.

Until then, I continued to do well academically and made the minimum effort necessary to get good GCSE results. But once I entered Sixth Form, things began to deteriorate. I'm certain that, from my parent's point of view, I was a very difficult teenager, when – from my perspective – I was merely determined to be my own person. While claiming they only had my well-being at heart, they refused to listen to what I had to say, or what I wanted to do. I responded accordingly, and my first tattoo – albeit very small and hidden at the base of my spine – was an act of rebellion. There were others.

Once my sister and I were teenagers, we ostensibly ate our meals as a family, but I rarely liked what Mum prepared and no longer sought either parent's approval.

'What are you doing?' Mum would ask as I put a saucepan of water on the hotplate on my return from school.

'Pasta.'

I knew she was asking for more of an explanation while I was unwilling to provide one.

Acts such as these were emotional timebombs that ticked for several years. The explosion came towards the end of school, during the millennium, in 2000. It was then I committed my ultimate act of rebellion. I fell pregnant.

Despite my relationship with Mum and Dad being at rock bottom, I was still afraid of telling them that I was going to have a baby. Instead, I wrote a letter that I hid… waiting for the right moment to deliver it. That moment never came because my parents found it when searching my room. They justified their invasion of my privacy as they 'suspected' something was wrong with me, but couldn't work out what it was. Unsurprisingly, I was furious and presumed it wasn't the first time they'd gone through my things. While I don't remember much of the detail from the almighty argument that followed, my decision to continue with the pregnancy was deemed *unacceptable*.

I have always been strongly pro-choice and support any woman's decision to have an abortion for whatever reason she decides. After all, it is her body. I find it particularly insulting when a man, who will never know the physical demands of pregnancy, childbirth, or lactation, pronounces on the morality of abortion. But, for myself, even while still at school and discovering the reality of morning sickness, I knew it wasn't what I wanted to do. Whatever the consequences, I was going to have a baby and give it the best possible life I could.

My parents disagreed.

'You'll not have a child in this house!', 'What a waste of a good education!', 'You're only a child yourself!', 'You've no idea what it takes to be a decent mother!', 'What kind of future can you offer a child?', 'You'll never amount to anything.'

Such anger and contempt served no purpose.

I wasn't massively surprised by their reaction or by their hurtful comments. At the same time, I was sure they were wrong. I wasn't just determined to be okay without them; I somehow knew I was going to have a great life. As would the baby growing inside me.

Looking back, I wonder if getting pregnant was actually an attempt to get out of an unhappy situation. My parents disapproved of my boyfriend, while I wanted to be with him all the time. Dan was the love of my life, and I could only see happiness ahead if we were together.

Rather than offer me support, the school I'd attended since the age of seven was embarrassed by my pregnancy and didn't know how to deal with it. Initially, in the hope I'd change my mind about having a baby, my parents threatened to withhold the final term's fees. Instead, when they realised that wasn't going to happen, they told me to leave home. Then my school announced all exam revision would have to be done at home – the one I'd just been ordered to leave!

For a while, I was tempted to walk away from it all, but with just a few months left before my A-Levels, I knew I'd regret being so impulsive. I could have taken the exams at the local college, but when my parents withdrew their threat, I stayed put. I took my A-Levels as planned, although the school arranged that I sit them in a classroom on my own. It was as if they thought pregnancy was contagious.

'Be careful to stay away from Alice.' I can almost hear the Head of Sixth Form's voice. 'Just to be on the safe side. We don't want your tummies growing too.' I remember the woman well and her high nasal tone. We all tried to keep our distance when she spoke due to the dreadful smell of her breath.

I was delighted to finally leave school, but at seven months pregnant, I'd already had more than a taste of what it means to be an independent adult. Since leaving home, I'd been working as a waitress, as well as studying as much as I could. I was quickly learning what was important. Morning sickness still plagued me, but my biggest concern was whether Dan and I would have a home of our own before the baby was born.

Dan wasn't much older than me but had worked as a plasterer since leaving school at 16. He was employed on a large construction project when my parents threw me out, and with nowhere else to go, we ended up living on the building site for several weeks. It was in one of the portable buildings that made up the workmen's quarters. Living and sleeping in one tiny room that was impossible to keep clean with barely any furniture and almost no privacy wasn't fun. The bathroom facilities were beyond a joke.

The closest loo to our room was known as 'the shithouse' for good reason. Resembling a grey plastic sentry box, it had an opaque Perspex roof that – while permitting daylight to enter –was pitch black at night. Dan argued this partly explained the coating of excrement in the toilet bowl and around the rim. It was evident that neither the manual flush, akin to a bilge pump, nor the small handbasin were often used.

'Do you reckon your workmates leave such a mess at home?' I asked him when first introduced to the shithouse.

'I don't suppose so,' he answered sheepishly, as if embarrassed that he hadn't noticed the stinking crud before

I pointed it out. It made me wonder whether groups of men, left to their own devices, explained the 'missing link' between modern *Homo sapiens* and the Neanderthals.

I became adept at using spray bleach whenever I entered the shithouse as well as the adjacent shower cubicle. That, too, was frequently adorned with traces of human waste.

If I wasn't working in the café, I'd collect my books together and spend the day in the public library until I knew the builders had finished for the day. With no reasonable alternative, we stayed until the sectioned buildings were taken down to be transported to another site miles away.

By then, we'd approached the Local Authority and were on a waiting list for a flat through a housing association. Unable to pay the cost of private renting, we returned to the Council when the building site moved to see what they could suggest. We were pleased when they told us we could stay in a local hostel until something became available. I'm not sure what I expected, but thought anywhere would be better than the building site.

I was wrong.

The hostel was on a main street, not far from the railway station where we stored our bags. From the outside, it was just another of the city's large Georgian houses. It could have been smarter but wasn't rundown either – others along the same terrace were small hotels or flats with a shop on the ground floor.

Dan and I were hopeful on the bright, sunny day when we crossed the road from the station and walked towards the address we'd been given. As we approached the building, I started to feel more anxious; angry shouts emanated from inside and a young guy was sprawled across the entrance. Thin and unshaven with reddish hair, his worn jeans had parted company with his sweatshirt to reveal a milky white stomach. We stepped over him to gain entry, but he took no notice and seemed blissfully unaware of the screaming.

The outside of the hostel may not have looked much different to any of its neighbours, but inside it was awful. After the front door closed on its hinges, leaving the bright sunshine behind, it was as if we'd entered a dark cave. We were all alone except for whoever was evidently very pissed off and very nearby.

The noise abruptly stopped, and a door to our right flung open.

'Who are you then?' Still a bark, but at a lower volume, we now discovered the angry voice belonged to the warden, Mike. He was small and round but with such wild hair that, along with a very bushy beard, he reminded me of Mufasa from The Lion King. Otherwise, he was almost as scruffy as the guy on the doorstep but, attentive to what we had to say, visibly calmed within a few moments. Once we'd finished explaining, he stepped into the corridor and closed the door behind him.

'Let me show you around.'

He looked at my growing belly before leading the way down the passage. 'It's probably not what you're used to,' he said, 'but at least it's somewhere for the time being.'

Reaching further along the dark interior, I could feel the baby twisting around inside me; it seemed to be moving in sympathy with my thumping heart. I'd suffered from morning sickness throughout the pregnancy, and my growing unease was making me nauseous. We came into a sizeable kitchen where the smell of rancid butter and cooking oil added to my discomfort. Breathing slowly through my mouth, I looked around at the kitchen units running the length of the room on either side with padlocks fitted to each cupboard door. Directly opposite me were two sash windows looking onto a brick wall with a sink under each. I knew the weather was beautiful outside but couldn't see even a patch of blue sky. From the encrusted sludge on the cooker hobs to the piles of dirty dishes alongside and the grease lines around the sinks, the place was disgusting. The soles of my shoes clung stickily to the vinyl flooring with each step.

'I'll work out which of these cupboards are free,' Mike waved towards the units. 'You're entitled to one each. Mind you, there's a deposit to pay for the locks. And you can use either fridge…' He hesitated for a moment. 'I wouldn't advise leaving too much in case someone else feels a bit peckish…' He walked on. 'And over here is the health and safety notice…'

I tried to make eye contact with Dan, but he was concentrating on the list of rules and fire regulations pinned beside a red hydrant on the lime-green wall. Mike was going through them one at a time.

I coughed.

Neither of them noticed, and I coughed again until Mike looked around, raising his bushy eyebrows in response.

'What about the cleaning?' I asked.

Mike continued to look at me while his eyebrows dropped back into the general mane covering his face.

'Who's responsible for keeping the kitchen clean? I asked again.

Both guys looked at the space around them as if they hadn't noticed the filth. Eventually, Mike replied cheerfully. 'Well, we do encourage everyone to muck in and do their bit. So, you're most welcome to give it a thorough mop and polish. If that's what you enjoy.' He beamed at me before turning to Dan.

'I'm sure your young lady will do a fine job,' he chuckled. 'It's just not something us men are very good at, is it?'

Dan made no comment.

At 18, I was still formulating my opinion of society and women's place within it. But I already knew men like Mike would have no place in my world. And I was browned off Dan had so little to say.

The more I saw of the hostel, the more I could see how poorly it was managed. The guy on the doorstep wasn't the only person we saw who was off his head. Everywhere was dirty, and oversized traps tucked under radiators indicated a problem that was larger than mice. It wasn't just the state of the place that I found so disturbing, but some of the tenants were also quite scary. I knew I could never stay there, and after we left, Dan agreed. The problem was we didn't have anywhere else to go.

Returning to the station for our bags, Dan told me to wait while he made a phone call. Sitting with pretty much all my worldly possessions in the ticket hall of Bath railway station, I didn't know whether to laugh or cry. Thankfully, Dan soon came back with a broad grin on his face.

'Gran's come up trumps!'

He started to gather our belongings, explaining that his grandmother had agreed to put us up. After helping me with the smaller of two rucksacks, Dan carried the rest of our belongings. We left the railway station and headed towards a nearby bus stop.

'Just make sure you're gone before that bun's out of the oven,' Dan's Gran told me when we got to her council house on the edge of the city. 'The last thing I need at my time of life is to be kept awake at night by a screaming baby.'

I continued to waitress part-time, but having Dan's granny's place gave me the chance to do some worthwhile revision before my exams. We were still living with her when I sat my A-Levels in June 2000. By then, however, we were starting to outstay our welcome, although it was another two months before we got the keys to somewhere for ourselves. It was a small two-bedroom flat on the ground floor of one of the city's few tower blocks, on quite a rough estate. But it was central and, most importantly, offered us somewhere permanent that was warm, vermin-free, and ours!

A fortnight later, we were joined by Lydia.

3. Building a Career as a Single Mother

As any parent will tell you, nothing can prepare you for the onslaught of love and raw emotion that a new child brings. And, as any mother will tell you, childbirth has to be the most physically painful experience women endure, and by far the most rewarding. After countless hours of agony, the moment that tiny pink bundle of Lydia was placed into my arms, I knew I'd adore her forever.

We were now a family, but Dan and I were still teenagers, and life was very tough. Most of our few items of furniture were given to us by Dan's granny or her friends, and we bought other bits second-hand after Lydia was born. Alex Lucas, a school friend and budding artist, painted a beautiful bright mural across one of Lydia's bedroom walls. It was her first large project and a forerunner to her future success.

Throughout this time, I didn't know anyone else with a young child. Lydia was the very first baby I had ever held, and like most first-time mothers, I didn't have an inkling about looking after her or breastfeeding. If I'd been aware of how painful feeding would be in those early weeks, and had a bit more cash, I'm sure she would have been bottle-fed!

Working as a junior plasterer, Dan didn't make much money, and once Lydia arrived, I had to figure out how we were going to survive financially. While further education was always on my horizon as a route to financial stability, earning more in the short term became a priority. So, within a couple of months of giving birth, I started working shifts in a local nightclub. I'd get home at 3 am and grab a few hours of sleep before getting up again to look after Lydia when Dan went to work. It was exhausting. We were still living hand to mouth, and I felt lonely during the daytime, but we weren't unhappy. Just tired and extremely poor!

Dan knew I wanted to continue my education, and I knew I needed a degree. To me, it was important if I wanted to build any sort of career and have financial security. Options were limited, partly due to my A-Level grades and partly because I didn't want to relocate. Fortunately, Bath University had a good reputation, and I found a course that sounded interesting – Sociology with Human Resource Management. When I gained a place to start, the year after Lydia was born, I grabbed the opportunity.

The admissions system wasn't as flexible as I'd expected. Instead of asking questions about my situation, it automatically assessed me as dependent on my parents. This meant I was charged full tuition fees and could only claim the minimum student loan. In addition, students weren't eligible for state benefits, and I needed to pay nursery fees. Once the course started, though, I went to the student finance office to get some help. I really wanted to concentrate on my degree but had no idea how I was going to afford it.

I practically lived at that office during Freshers Week.

'Bring in a mug tomorrow,' Karen, one of the assistants who tottered around on red stilettos, told me after the second day. 'That way, you can enjoy a cuppa while seeing what's what.' I did as I was told and was amazed by how methodical, thorough and single-minded she was in helping me work through countless spreadsheets and forms that explored funding options.

'Your name should be Erin, not Karen,' I told her. 'Like Erin Brockovich – the Julia Roberts film. You even look like her.'

She laughed, 'I wish!'

Finally, we – or rather she – managed to scrape together enough emergency funding applications to make it possible for me to continue studying, as long as I continued working part-time.

I loved being a student. The course was varied and just as interesting as I'd hoped. It felt great being able to use my brain again, and throwing myself into the mix, I devoured the learning opportunity and made some good friends. Although barely older than those around me, due to being a mum, I was often treated as the wise older sister. So different from the *persona non grata* I'd become at school less than two years earlier.

Although supportive beforehand, almost from the day I started, Dan was unhappy about what university life involved and our relationship began to sour. Each morning, he'd ask for my whereabouts for the day and would later check to see if anything had changed. He grew increasingly insecure about what I was doing and who I was meeting. Excuses were created to prevent me from going somewhere without him while, simultaneously, he refused to come anywhere with me. I was still waitressing and doing bar shifts, so there was barely time for a social life, but Lydia was embraced by my fellow students and I wanted to get involved in what I could.

As I entered my second year, my relationship with Dan deteriorated as he became more controlling. Even when he knew I had a work shift or lecture to attend (by this time, I'd pinned a weekly timetable to the kitchen wall), there would be incessant questions and delaying tactics. 'Where are you off to this time?', 'I thought you weren't working Friday evenings any more', 'Can you check there's a clean babygro/enough nappies/milk in the fridge before you go?'

If I wanted to use the car we'd bought, he'd find a more pressing need for it. Lydia would be blamed for misplacing the car keys that would turn up when it was too late for me to leave. Once, when I couldn't find my wallet, Dan refused to lend me £5. 'Sorry, babe, I spent my last fiver on petrol.' I found the wallet back in my bag as I got ready for bed that night.

For a long time, I was too busy to stop and think whether or not Dan's behaviour was reasonable and did my very best to keep him happy. Even if I wasn't. As if on autopilot, I took on the subordinate female role I'd been brought up with. At the same time, my ideas were expanding through my studies, discovering different pathways through sociology and psychology. Reading masses of books, and keen to learn, I began to understand how society perpetuates the myth that men should dominate women. It still took me two years to acknowledge that my relationship with Dan was so unhealthy that I'd had enough of it.

My third year at university was a full-time work placement, and I fought tooth and nail to make sure I got one of the very few that were paid. It offered a proper salary that allowed me the freedom to make my own decisions. Meanwhile, my relationship with Dan had – finally – broken down completely. Lydia was three when I left him, and I vowed no man would ever control my life in that way again.

Dan knew our relationship had failed but didn't take it well. Along with threatening to kill me, and slashing my car's brand-new tyres, he swore I'd never be safe in public again. He then walked out of our lives as if we'd never existed. I have never received a penny in child support, and neither Lydia nor I have had anything to do with him since.

So, here I stood – a 21-year-old single mum on a work placement, starting my career in human resources. At the modest salary of £12,000, I was very pleased with where I was, though.

The future felt bright.

Once I completed my degree, I started working for the HR team in a local hospital. Along with a moderate salary increase, I was also able to enrol for a postgraduate diploma in HR to assist in future promotion and give me a greater understanding of the industry. Given the solid work ethic and desire for good that seemed to permeate through the NHS, I've never understood why its administration is forever pilloried in our media and by many of our politicians. One manager made a point of coming into the hospital on a Sunday afternoon to make sure elderly patients – who otherwise wouldn't have a visitor – at least saw him for a few minutes. Until they got to know him better, new members of staff assumed he had a large number of elderly relatives who happened to be in hospital at the same time.

Lydia continued to thrive, and once my working day was over I loved the time we spent together. But, like an itch that constantly needs to be scratched, something was missing from my life. No matter how widely I read, or how much I studied, I couldn't find the intellectual fulfilment I craved from my job. In turn, I'd inadvertently joined a profession perceived as particularly *appropriate* for women. How did that happen!?

I'm not sure why I chose to change career and move into law. My dad was a lawyer, so maybe it was a subconscious decision to do something I'd grown up to believe was a man's job. Maybe I wanted to show my parents that I was equal to my father – or any man. Whatever the reason, it wasn't going to be an easy transition, but my mind was made up. I knew I would do whatever it took to achieve my ambition.

'Look out world,' I thought. 'Here I come!'

The GDL started just a couple of weeks later. However, with such demand for every place, merely to be considered for an assessment day meant I had to meet rigorous application criteria. Despite my good degree result and postgraduate HR qualification, I soon found out that my poor A-Levels ruled me out of the majority. I couldn't apply to the most prestigious firms, but – after some painstaking research into which companies would consider me – I chose where to target and to make sure the graduate recruitment managers in each of those firms knew who I was.

'Hello,' I'd reach forward to shake hands with the recruiters on their stands at career fairs, 'I'm Alice.'

While squirming with discomfort at being so pushy, I'd make sure we locked eyes before enthusing about how much I'd love to work for them. I ensured I had full contact details before moving on to the next law firm.

Afterwards, I would follow up with emails, and if I didn't get a response, I picked up the phone. Where necessary, I rang the firms' HR departments to find out who I needed to speak to and called directly. I wanted to explain why I didn't get the A-Level grades I should have accomplished without telling them I was a mum. It didn't occur to me that getting an excellent degree while being a single parent to a young child was an achievement in itself! I felt my early pregnancy would make me look bad, so I kept it to myself.

Ultimately, I don't think the recruitment managers cared why I didn't get the grades – they had more than enough applicants. On the contrary, my A-Levels offered an easy excuse to avoid looking further into my submission. It wasn't a great experience to effectively make a nuisance of myself, but I still think I was right to do everything I could to shift the odds more in my favour. And, if nothing else, it gave me a smidgen of confidence in myself that I was able to take forward.

After chasing graduate recruitment managers and completing a dozen application forms, I waited. The first rejection arrived almost by return of email, and others soon followed. Eventually, I made it onto the waiting list of just one firm's assessment day, and although it wasn't from a top firm, Rease & Able was well-respected. I'd been rapidly rebuffed by all of the others.

After all my efforts, I felt seriously deflated. Getting onto a single waiting list was all I'd achieved. I began to wonder if I could have done more and – at this point, in August 2007 – I'd actually handed my notice in with the NHS because the GDL started the following month.

Then, exactly one week before the assessment day, a woman from Rease & Able rang to let me know someone had dropped out.

'We wondered if you are still interested in attending?' she asked. 'It's next Friday.'

'Definitely!' I declared. I was still in with a chance! 'I'll be there.'

'Excellent. It starts promptly at 9 am. Let's hope it goes well for you,' she replied. 'I look forward to meeting you next Friday, Alice.'

I could see my hand shaking as I hung up on the call. My whole future career hinged on 'next Friday'.

Despite my HR background and broad understanding of the assessment process, I didn't have a clue about how well I might do and as Friday approached, I became increasingly nervous. I knew I had to make it work, but I didn't know how. Then, on the Thursday evening, I discovered the school holiday care scheme for Lydia had been cancelled for the following day. Putting my nerves to one side, I scrambled around to find someone able to help me out at short notice.

I took a long hot shower early on the Friday morning and dressed carefully. I didn't want to look the same as everyone else, but I also didn't want to take too much of a risk. I settled on a cream and brown pinstripe skirt suit from Karen Millen.

Leaving Lydia with another mum from school, I gave her a hug and drove across to Bristol with my stomach doing more somersaults than an Olympic gymnast. I knew that becoming a lawyer depended on me performing, and I couldn't let myself down. I arrived at Rease & Able's reception desk in good time, was offered a seat, and took a few long, deep breaths before I saw a woman approaching from a rear doorway. She was about ten years older than me and dressed in a short-sleeved summer frock. I assumed she wasn't a lawyer.

'I'm so pleased to meet you, Alice.' She smiled warmly. 'I'm Rachel. We spoke last week.'

I returned the smile.

'Are you ready?' she asked.

I was as ready as I was ever going to be.

Back at work on the Monday, I checked my inbox regularly, praying there wouldn't be a rejection email waiting. The assessment day had been long and involved psychometric tests, group exercises, presentations and interviews. The other candidates were obviously a few years younger than me. I'd given everything my best shot.

My mobile rang, and the number was familiar.

Big gulp.

'Good news, Alice,' were Rachel's first words.

I started to cry.

Rease & Able's training contract meant I could feed and clothe Lydia as well as go and study for two years. Travelling from Bath to Bristol daily was pretty intense, but I threw myself into learning, loved it all and did well. With Rachel's generous help, I also got some hands-on experience by working in a secretarial capacity for Rease & Able during the holidays, which earned some much-needed extra cash.

When I finished the GDL and LPC in 2009, businesses in every industry were still suffering from the previous year's economic freefall. Legal firms across the country were deferring training contracts because they had effectively hired two years in advance and now lacked work for the trainees coming through. Some of my fellow students were more than happy to be offered a lump sum of money in the knowledge they could go off travelling and return a year or two later to a guaranteed training contract. For me, it was different. It was time to earn a proper salary. 'Please don't defer my training contract,' I said to Rachael, 'I have to start work.' I was one of just four trainees that year – about half the size of a normal training intake.

In those days, the two-year training contract was quite rigid and firms offered a six-month period in four different areas of law or 'seats'. Under a supervisor, I was involved in as much variety of work as possible within that seat. I also needed to keep a detailed record of exactly what I did – and my points of reference for what I learned – to ensure there was a thorough and complete register of everything I covered. It was essentially a method of continual assessment being signed off by a supervisor at regular intervals (and again at the end of the six months) to agree that requirements had been met. There was no final exam.

More recently, the Solicitors Regulation Authority broadened the methods of becoming a solicitor, and a fixed two-year contract with one firm is becoming less common. Its replacement is a 'Period of Recognised Training'. This still covers various areas of law with detailed training records but can be done part-time over several years with different 'seats' in different firms. If you haven't taken the LPC, you now have the option of taking the Solicitors Qualifying Examination (SQE). Although a positive move offering a more flexible approach, it remains tough, competitive and expensive to train and qualify as a solicitor.

Even before I began law school, I knew which areas most interested me and I was fortunate Rease & Able was largely able to accommodate them. My previous HR experience taught me that I preferred finding out how to help businesses thrive rather than delving into people's personal lives to help individuals in their private affairs. Sifting through someone else's dirty laundry wasn't for me, and I'm not sure how well I could have represented a negligent parent.

I did seats in Corporate Banking and Insolvency, Professional Negligence, Property Litigation and Commercial Contracts.

Life was busier than ever and it was wonderful. My work was challenging but rewarding, my colleagues were fun to be with, my progress and accumulation of knowledge could almost be measured by the day. At the same time, I could see that – as a working mum – reaching the upper echelons of the legal profession wasn't going to be a straightforward climb. If I wanted to rise, I needed to fit into the mould of my male peers, predecessors who'd moved up the ladder, and partners who'd reached the top rung. As in other corporate professions, women were expected to dress in the female equivalent of a man's suit and I made sure to keep my couple of small tattoos hidden under my shirt sleeves. This type of conformity was already frustrating, but I told myself to simply put my head down, get on with the job at hand, and do it well.

It wasn't long after settling back into full-time work that I met the person without whom Stephenson Law would not exist.

Pete and I had been at law school together but only got to know each other later through a mutual friend. When we met, he was a professional poker player who ran a successful online poker school. He was the first person I knew – in my generation – who ran his own business. Until then, I'd been surrounded by people who wanted to be lawyers, doctors or accountants. Until Pete, I hadn't come across anyone who wanted to beat their own path, make their own money and do things a little differently.

He looked different too, and was evidently not shy about body art. Although I'd added to my original 'tramp stamp', I couldn't imagine being so bold. Both of Pete's arms, his chest, ribs and back were heavily inked.

'Did you show them at law school?' I asked, thinking about how carefully I kept my own discreet tattoos covered.

'Of course,' he replied. 'They're an important part of who I am. Why shouldn't I show them?'

Thinking of the lecturers, all dyed-in-the-wool besuited lawyers, I couldn't help but laugh. Which planet did this guy come from? He certainly wasn't from my world.

'Well, I'm not surprised you didn't finish the course,' I said.

'I didn't leave because of what I look like.' Pete looked straight into my eyes. 'It just didn't mean enough to me to fit in.'

For the first time in my life, I knew I was talking to someone about big things that mattered to me. Things that he understood. We'd only just met and – while I know it's a cliché to admit this – it really was as if we'd known each other forever.

In those very early days of being a lawyer, I was determined to do whatever it took to be successful. I was only just discovering the archaic restrictions of the industry and felt sure I'd find a way to break through any barriers. Others thought I was aiming too high, whereas Pete told me, 'Of course you can do it. Why not?' From our first date, he has always been my biggest supporter. Without Pete, I would never have considered starting my own legal firm. It wasn't even on my radar.

Running a business was never discussed at school, and looking at my parents and their friends, it wasn't something that crossed their minds either. Entrepreneurship and becoming a business leader is a degree option today, but even working for yourself wasn't considered a serious career goal in the world I grew up in.

Pete looked at things differently, though. Our relationship became serious quite quickly, and I felt my outlook was rapidly changing, too. Until then, and in every environment I'd been in – whether that was at home or school or work – I lacked confidence. I felt I couldn't meet people's expectations of what I should look like, behave like or think. I always felt that there was something wrong with me. That I simply wasn't good enough. I didn't know at the time, but it was a classic case of imposter syndrome.

Pete changed all of that. He persuaded me otherwise: that I looked great; that I should behave as I wanted; that thinking outside the box was good; that I was good; and that if I wanted to do anything strongly enough, I could.

His faith in my ability was magically eye-opening for me. We were soon talking about marriage and it seemed the most natural thing in the world for me to share his surname.

In contrast to what my parents expected, Pete has always been there for Lydia, too. Rather than being put off by me being a single mum, he was fully on board. Of course, Lydia's biological dad wasn't around, so he was able to be a proper father for her. From the beginning, Pete has always been her only dad.

Before we got married, we fell pregnant with our son, Adam, during the second year of my training contract. Determined that his birth wouldn't affect my career trajectory, I took just four months of maternity leave as it wouldn't affect my qualifying date. Very conscious of being older than most of my contemporaries, I was in a rush to become a fully-fledged solicitor. In hindsight, a few months here or there would have made no difference, so I regretted going back to work so quickly. Pete, working from home, took on the major share of childcare, and I finished my training in September 2011.

The economy was still recovering from the 2009 crash, and a phone call during our honeymoon in Devon informed me that Rease & Able couldn't offer me a permanent role in my chosen area of contract law. They simply didn't have any jobs. So, as I approached qualifying, I reluctantly started to apply to other law firms for a job.

Of course, it wasn't just Rease & Able who had few jobs. The legal job market at the time was horrendously difficult, and I had an additional challenge… there is a stigma attached to a newly-qualified solicitor who *isn't* kept on by the firm that has just paid to train them. It's automatically assumed that the solicitor is lacking in some way, either no good or unreliable.

Fortunately, Rease & Able gave me glowing references and put me directly in touch with other firms to help overcome that stigma. I was genuinely sad to leave them, and it was the only firm I've worked for that treated its staff as people with characters and lives outside the office rather than insensitive automatons. I sometimes wonder what would have happened if they'd had a job for me on qualification…

Instead, in September 2011, I trotted off on my first day as a qualified solicitor to a new firm. Lydia cantered happily into her final year at primary school, and Adam, keen to chew on anything he could reach, was just about onto all fours. Knowing Pete would always be around if any of us had a wobble, I held my head high as I approached the offices of KWS, Knotte Wirthey Solicitors.

5. Love the Work but not the Workplace

Walking into KWS on that Monday morning, I was hoping for a similar degree of understanding and support to the one I'd experienced at Reese & Able. Instead, it was evident from the word go that Knotte Wirthey was only interested in the amount of work I could take on, and how much I could bill clients each month. Adverts in Bristol's glossy lifestyle magazines gave the firm a veneer of quality and dependability due to its long history with the city; readers would barely have noticed it was a business aiming to make money and certainly not one where bonanza drawings for equity partners was its main goal.

There was no acknowledgement within the firm that I, or any other KWS lawyer, was a real person. A human being with a character, strengths and weaknesses. Someone who needs to be encouraged and appreciated to give of their best.

At the same time, having only just qualified as a solicitor, it was very hard to gauge what was reasonable for me to anticipate. I'd been warned it would be a shock stepping up from being a trainee. Expectations increase – as does the workload – and I was in a different firm, among different people. Nevertheless, there was a lot of pressure, and despite working alongside some lovely people, I felt out of my depth. Any misgivings I had at Reese & Able about how someone like me could succeed in the legal world rapidly grew. Frankly, I felt like a rabbit in headlights.

Part of the problem was my growing awareness that the whole industry was generally out of synch with the 21st century. It seemed to be stuck somewhere in the Mad Men era of 1960s advertising, or perhaps earlier still, when everything was monochrome. I could see how law firms' marketing strategies, rather than highlighting specific areas of excellence, were boringly homogenous. Without any sign of a USP, other than perhaps suggesting they'd been around since the wheel was invented and were equally reliable, they were trying to be everything to everyone and cause offence to no one. There was no acknowledgement that while this strategy wouldn't offend, it wouldn't interest either. It wouldn't differentiate one firm from another.

This insistence on uniformity filtered down to every department and explained why I hid my tattoos, even though I was unhappy having to hide parts of my personality. When I went to work each morning, it was as if I had to paint myself grey at the door. If, by chance, I was wearing a blouse that showed a tattoo, I knew someone would be ready to make a snarky comment. And yet how could this outward signal of *who I was* adversely affect the quality of my work? On the contrary, I felt sure I would be more productive if I was comfortable in being myself, rather than projecting this non-being cloaked in dreariness.

Having to act like a KWS automaton was just one of several issues I struggled to accept.

Another was being employed as part of a team with two sub-divisions. The difference between the two wasn't about areas of experience or expertise. Instead, it was all about gender. I worked alongside female lawyers while the other sub-division was entirely male. Tom – the partner in charge of us all – then decided which client we would be sent to work with, and in what capacity.

Most law firms give each of their lawyers a target of billable hours to reach each month. Partners and senior lawyers chase and win accounts for themselves and junior lawyers to work on. Most of the senior partners at KWS were men, and while this shouldn't have affected the career chances of women like me, I knew it did. In any case, along with my colleagues, I relied on Tom to give me the work in order for me to build the requisite billable hours to reach my monthly target. I had no input on which jobs came my way, and if Tom didn't pass me enough to do, I couldn't make my target. This rarely happened, but I felt it unfair for anyone to be given a monthly target that could be impossible to achieve for reasons beyond their control, particularly when so much value was placed on hitting the target. Not giving someone enough work while expecting them to account for enough billable hours each month was like asking a chef to cook a three-course meal while only providing the ingredients for two.

As the most junior member of my team, and being aware that it was unusual to have moved firms immediately on qualifying, I didn't utter a word about what I saw as injustices. During my early months at KWS, I didn't put a foot wrong either. I dressed impeccably and, not wanting motherhood to be an impediment, relied heavily on Pete for our childcare needs. I was very ambitious, wanted promotion and kept my head down with my nose to the grindstone. Even so, it wasn't long before I overheard a conversation that made me question whether I would ever realise my dream career in law.

Becky was one of my more senior female colleagues and a mum who, despite being 'part-time', put in endless hours (including on her non-working days) and was a brilliant lawyer. We'd returned to the office together one day after finishing a contract review with a client, and she approached our boss Tom's desk.

'How did you get on?' he asked.

'Absolutely fine, no problems at all,' she replied. 'I just wanted to check you're okay if I leave early on Thursday to catch the end of my daughter's sports day.'

'Really?' The inflexion in Tom's voice was either sarcastic or incredulous. 'You want time off to watch a bunch of kids run round the park?'

'If you want, I can come back to the office afterwards,' Becky said. 'Although you can see it looks like I've already got this month's target nailed.'

'I'd much rather see it looking like you were getting a nanny instead of skipping off early,' Tom sighed before turning away to answer his phone.

Becky waited a moment before walking across to sit at her desk. She seemed pensive while reaching to turn on her computer screen but made no comment. An excellent, experienced lawyer who was popular with clients, she handed her notice in to KWS just a few days later.

Given Pete's flexibility and 'can do' attitude with business, I was already keen to work for myself (although this was long before Stephenson Law was even a fantasy, let alone something I considered a realistic possibility). Instead, while doing everything I could to succeed as a junior lawyer, I decided to set up an online business as a side hustle.

Along the lines of Etsy or Not on the High Street, it offered a marketplace to creators of quality hand-made wedding accessories. Working late into evenings and weekends, I approached suppliers, built the website, and ran it for about a year. I loved doing something over which I had control, that seemed worthwhile and where I could be myself.

It was all hunky-dory until I realised my business model was fundamentally flawed. It wasn't making any money! I'd hit a problem common to new entrepreneurs in not knowing how to value the service being offered. I managed to sell the business and recoup some of my losses but, back in my day job with KWS, I discovered the structure that held me back from career advancement wasn't always good for clients either.

While the billable hours system was supposed to be an incentive for lawyers to be assiduous and produce financial results, it was also an inducement for an unethical lawyer to cheat.

Cheating came in countless guises, depending on where the lawyer was in their career. I heard of one senior partner who thought it reasonable to include his Sunday afternoon rounds of golf with a client's CEO, and another who clocked time spent at a charity dinner he attended with his wife because it was sponsored by an important client. Although the hourly rates of both men would have been extortionately high, their clients were equally high value and I can only assume the additional costs were lost in the maelstrom of the companies' extensive legal bills.

Further down the pecking order, I knew of a partner who occasionally undertook work that should have been done by a more junior member of staff. He then padded out his hours with the justification that a less experienced lawyer would have taken longer to complete the project. When I queried this with a colleague, I was assured such an explanation was reasonable. Another dodgy excuse for registering an additional hour or two each month was for 'thinking time'. Although this was generally frowned upon, if it happened when perhaps the lawyer was on his daily commute or even taking a shower, if *written notes* of those thoughts were made later the *same* day, the thinking time could be included.

On a more mundane level, most law firms structure their billing procedures in six-minute chunks, which means that even the briefest of phone conversations with a senior partner can cost close to £100. I witnessed many occasions when a lawyer would ask after a client's health or recent holiday to lengthen a call so that a six-minute increment would be added to their billable hours. And it was as likely to be a senior lawyer as a junior. I saw how the 'carrot and stick' argument, where the only value given to lawyers was fiscal, created a toxic culture. I despised a system that couldn't appreciate how, as human beings, giving of our best is not necessarily consistent and how – during one month – we are able to give more than the following. Or vice versa.

Now that I run my own business, I am in a position where I appreciate how every member of staff has to pull their financial weight, but I also know there are better ways than bullying to get the most out of people. Despite being less naïve than when I was a newly qualified solicitor, I still believe encouraging people to be dishonest in the hours they've worked – to avoid potential consequences should they miss an arbitrary monthly target – is fundamentally wrong.

Although I didn't approve of a lot that was going on around me, I had to be a part of it, and found a wry satisfaction in the name of Knotte Wirthey being so apt. I also found the demands required to draft and review commercial contracts both challenging and rewarding. A lot of my time was spent in clients' offices, where I was involved in complex projects that required thinking outside the box as well as comprehensive legal knowledge. These included international contracts for logistics companies and health organisations, as well as finicky franchise agreements for telecoms. The satisfaction I found in my daily occupation didn't alter my low opinion of KWS, though, and after about 18 months I was keen to move on to a different firm. This was pretty much the legal industry's minimum length of employment that was deemed acceptable on a CV.

It wasn't long before I found another job doing similar work within a different sector. It offered a pay rise commensurate with added responsibility and, once again, I trotted off with my head held high and hoped my new employer would appreciate me as a worthy asset. It was early 2013, the year Lydia became a teenager and Adam hit the 'terrible twos'.

I began working for Blinkered Brothers without any idea of how important a move it was.

John Blinkered, who unwittingly helped germinate Stephenson Law a few years later, didn't even know who I was at this stage. Instead, I was working for Tim, one of the firm's younger partners.

As with KWS, I relied on Tim to feed me jobs. A substantial amount of my time with Blinkered Brothers involved SaaS, or Software as a Service, contracts. This is where there is a sale or purchase of software delivered in the Cloud rather than having it installed on a local computer or server. Technology was changing rapidly, with new software applications and pioneering innovations being created by the booming startup economy.

I had no problem with the scope of the work, which proved to be all-consuming and widely varied. My problem was that Blinkered Brothers didn't prove to be much better employers than KWS.

Relying on someone else to ensure I could reach my billable hours target each month still rankled, but I'd gotten used to it, and with an expanding knowledge base was generally confident in my ability to achieve what was demanded. While this didn't mean I could guarantee I'd always hit my target, my first issue with Blinkered Brothers wasn't personal. Instead, it was a perfect illustration of how the billable hours system can be used to undermine staff.

A monthly report of every lawyer's utilisation figures was circulated around the firm. Anyone who didn't hit 90% of their target had their names and figures highlighted in red. It wasn't about information sharing; it was a system of naming and shaming that I've come across since, and still struggle to understand how it can ever be justified in a civilised workplace.

My other issue was personal and partly due to the design of its open-plan office. Stretching across the whole floor of an office block, it had such low space dividers that everyone could see whoever got up and left their desk for whatever reason. As a result, I was once called to account for my recorded work hours.

I no longer relied on Pete for all the childcare all the time, and we took it in turns to collect Adam after work. The nursery closed at 6 pm, and it had been noticed I was often the first to leave the office at the end of the day.

'How are things going?' Tim asked while looking at his screen in front of him. I wasn't one of those demonised victims highlighted in red and wondered why he'd asked to see me.

'Alright,' I answered. 'Is there a problem?'

'Well,' he hesitated for a moment before continuing, 'someone who's been working on the Metcalf contract with you has suggested your hours don't really add up this month.'

Only one person worked with me at Metcalf and, as another junior lawyer, it was disappointing to think he'd questioned my integrity. He was also someone who had told me how 'thinking time' should, as a matter of course, be included in any lawyer's billable hours account.

'Given that I don't live with him, I'm surprised he has any idea about the hours I work,' I replied. 'I don't know what you do when you go home, Tim, but after having fed my kids and put them to bed, I log back into my laptop and do a few more hours pretty much every evening. If you doubt my word, I'm sure the IT department could confirm it for you.'

Ruffled and pink-cheeked, Tim muttered a half-apology and no more was said. Nevertheless, it made me realise that no matter how good a job I did, it would never be enough.

I'd never make partner in such a toxic environment where people had to vie with one another rather than be valued for what they achieved. The issue of 'presenteeism' versus 'absenteeism', where you had to be seen in an office for it to be acknowledged that you were working, was senseless to me. A few years later, when Covid hit, remote became normal for millions of people. Only then was it widely acknowledged how commonplace working from home already was for so many people, and the advantages this offered to both employer and employee.

Following Tim's questions, I waited for as long as necessary before looking to move on again. I saw that Barracuda, a large firm renowned for cutting-edge technology, was offering good salaries and had recently set up in Bristol.

On arrival at my new workplace and without even an hour's induction, I was handed a contract. Before having a chance to take a look, I was told to review it on the train to London, where I would meet with the client.

Apparently, every client was in London. The daily commute had not been mentioned during my interview. Barracuda had opened a Bristol office where good local salaries were still around 20% less than what lawyers earned in London, and when I was explicitly told not to tell clients I was from the Bristol office so they could charge me out at their London rates, alarm bells started ringing.

One of Barracuda's partners, a woman called Suella, has to be one of the most unpleasant people I've ever worked with. It came as no surprise to find out she was known as Cruella by almost everyone else in the company. Although another partner thought it appropriate to email me at midnight on a

Saturday (and again just four hours later), it was Suella who almost made me walk away from my legal career altogether.

After returning from a full day in London, I'd dropped some paperwork into the office and was heading for the door. It was already 7 o'clock and I knew I'd be lucky to see Adam before bedtime. Then I heard Suella's shrill voice calling me over to her desk, where she was hunched over a stack of papers. She didn't even look up to acknowledge my presence.

'I've got to review this contract.' This was 2014, and despite Barracuda's reputation, I saw she was still using pen and paper. 'Once I'm through, you need to scan it back to the London office.'

'You're asking me to wait while you review a contract so that I can scan it for you?' I just wanted to get home and spend some time with my family.

'Is that so difficult for you?' came her reply.

'Yes. It is,' I said. 'I'll show you how to use the scanner, but I won't wait to scan it for you.'

When she didn't answer, I left the office. I handed my notice in the next morning after just two weeks of employment.

I'd been so excited about working for Barracuda with its spearhead status. I'd put up with being sent to London on a Bristol salary that carved into every weekday evening. I'd put up with receiving emails through the night and even replied to one on a Sunday morning. But Cruella had wanted too big a slice of my life.

Or maybe she personified everything I hated about the industry. In any case, she made me question whether I was cut out to be a lawyer after all.

Defeated and deflated with summer approaching, I chose to take some time out. I needed to think what to do next. I needed to be me! I dyed my hair pink and loved being able to show my tattoos all day, every day, if I felt like it. I didn't have to 'paint myself grey' before going to work.

I felt liberated, and it was wonderful.

A couple of months later, I still had no idea what to do next, and while we just about managed on what Pete was earning, I was keen to start work again. Then, out of the blue, I got a phone call from Tim at Blinkered Brothers.

'I gather it didn't work out with Barracuda,' he said. 'So, I wondered if you fancied coming back?'

'Not really, Tim.' I answered truthfully. 'I just don't want to be a lawyer anymore. I want to be me.'

'Well, we've got a client who's specifically asking for you,' he said.

'But I can't go back to being a cog in your legal machine,' I replied.

'Why not freelance?'

Freelancing in the legal industry was quite common among more senior lawyers, but not for someone with only three years of experience, like me. It hadn't been something I'd considered. Even after Tim's call, I still thought it would be something for the short-term rather than a career move.

Initially, I was offered a day rate for a specific contract without any opportunity to negotiate the fee. It still meant I was earning more than I did as an employee, but the major gain was the emotional freedom. Working on contracts for different law firms and businesses, I started to feel less constrained by their rules. I could wear what I wanted and spend as many hours in the office as I chose to. I knew I was getting the work done and doing it well. As did others. Clients asked for me, and after about a year, I began to take more control of my daily rate.

This is when John Blinkered finally noticed me, and things started to fall into place. While I'd been his employee, I was invisible. He hadn't even registered my name. Once I became freelance – no longer stymied by the billable hours system or having to be present in the office – the quality of my work was noticed.

As long as the client was really happy with what I achieved, so was the law firm that hired me. As a result, more and more interesting opportunities came my way, including the Bull contract from John Blinkered. But when I became pregnant for the third time, we had our memorable meeting when John turned his back on me.

I met up with Tim a little after the meeting and explained what had happened. I'd been freelancing regularly for around three years by then and thought we knew each other quite well. I thought he was different from most of the male lawyers I worked with and understood me.

'Have you considered getting a nanny, Alice? he asked. 'That might sort your problems out.'

I raised my eyebrows. 'That's exactly what I overheard a Partner tell a female colleague at KWS a few years ago.'

'Well, he was right.' Tim was adamant. 'It's the only way a woman can have a family and a successful legal career. It's always been that way.'

'What?' I looked at Tim with a mix of scorn and pity.

He wasn't different after all.

The *only* way to have a family and a successful legal career is to pay someone else to bring up my kids? Screw that!

PART TWO – CREATION

6. The Need for Change

I knew that John Blinkered's attitude, and Tim's belief about mothers working as lawyers, were endemic across the industry. The problems I encountered trying to build a career while maintaining my identity as a woman and having a family were not unique. On researching this book, I discovered that the British legal profession is a long-established 'Old Boys' Club' with confusingly opaque yet clearly defined membership criteria.

Broadly speaking, a bright young law graduate who is male, white and privately educated will experience rapid career progression on a well-trodden route to becoming an equity partner in a prestigious law firm. As well as inherited wealth, he will have enjoyed an education available to less than 6% of the population, will speak RP – contemporary 'Received Pronunciation' – and will have benefitted from the expansive social network each of these bring. By contrast, an exceptionally gifted young law graduate who speaks with a regional accent and is a black woman will have to work a lot harder to make partner in any law firm or succeed as a barrister.

Tahina Akther is a family finance barrister who was called to the Bar in 2003. She is the daughter of Bangladeshi immigrants – her father was a steelworker, and she was educated at state schools. 'It can seem like a different world,' she says. 'I was part of this exclusive club… There was a bit of a feeling of imposter syndrome… Do I belong here?'[1]

The Bridge Group, a social equality organisation, found that promotion and the route to becoming a partner is largely dependent on being a protégé of a senior partner[2] who will oversee a trainee's progress and help create opportunities. Finding such a powerful advocate is usually only possible via

---

[1] Financial Times, 17 October 2022
[2] Bridge Group Report, 2020

social connections through family, school, or university and – even today – women rarely have such good fortune.

This was also part of the key findings in the InterLaw Diversity Forum's research carried out in 2021. Its opening paragraph states that since women were first permitted to practise law a century earlier, 'gender diversity and gender equality in the legal profession has been painfully slow'. It also lamented how little had changed since the Forum's first report a decade earlier. In the meantime, the constraints of the Covid pandemic had 'highlighted and exacerbated existing inequalities', resulting in more women reducing their work hours to cope with their caring responsibilities in the home. In other words, women continue to be held back in an industry they've been entitled to be a part of for more than 100 years.

Until then, female law graduates, even those with first class honours degrees, weren't permitted to qualify as solicitors or barristers. They had to wait for the Sex Disqualification (Removal) Act of 1919 to be allowed to train as teachers, accountants, barristers, and solicitors or be selected as jurors and magistrates for the first time.

As is evident from the Act's title, it became illegal to prevent someone from following a specific profession simply due to their gender. It is no coincidence that this followed World War One when the success of women's work in what had previously been seen as men's occupations was integral to the conflict's outcome.

The Act, while welcomed by the women's movement, didn't bring about equality, however, and 50% of the population could still be legally discriminated against by various means in the workplace. Professions like teaching maintained its insistence that female members of staff leave paid employment on marriage: 'The duty of a married woman is primarily to look after her domestic concerns and it is impossible for her to do so and to effectively and satisfactorily act as a teacher at the same time,' stated a British judge in 1925 when a Dorset schoolmistress attempted to challenge the law. The appeal court ruling continued by saying, 'It is unfair to the large number of young unmarried teachers seeking situations that the positions should be occupied by married women, who presumably have husbands capable of maintaining them.'

Some areas of the civil service, including the Foreign and Diplomatic offices, continued to exclude women altogether. Judges could still ask for them to be removed from juries on a whim, and it took another 50 years before a woman could demand the same pay for performing similar tasks to her brother, husband or father. This became law when the Equal Pay Act 1970 came into being, after a group of women machinists went on strike at Ford's Dagenham car factory.

'We're on the lowest rate of the entire bleeding factory despite the fact we got considerable skill,' Rita O'Grady, the strike leader, explained. 'And there's only one possible reason for that. It's 'cause we're women. And in the workplace, women get paid less than men, no matter what skill they got! Which is why from now on, we got to demand a level playing field and rates of pay which reflect the job you do, not whether you got a dick or not!'[3]

Even after O'Grady's plain speaking and the success of the Dagenham strike, it was another five years before discrimination on the grounds of gender or marriage was outlawed in the UK – more than half a century after the original Sex Disqualification Act allowed women to become lawyers.

---

[3] From the 2010 film 'Made in Dagenham'.

Born in Glasgow in 1896, Madge Easton Anderson was the first British female solicitor to qualify as a solicitor. The youngest of three daughters, Anderson came from a working class family and attended the local primary school in the city's suburb of Pollokshields, where her father was a medical instrument salesman. After winning a scholarship to a girls' grammar school that included a bursary to cover the cost of books, she later attended Glasgow University, graduating with an MA in 1916. That was when John Spens, a senior partner at Maclay, Murray & Spens LLP, probably suspecting that women would soon be allowed entry to the legal profession, offered her an apprenticeship.

Discovering that Anderson's application to practise was initially refused (because her training had begun before the 1919 Act) underlined to me how women lawyers have struggled to take their rightful place in the industry from the word go. Like any pioneer, Anderson was forthright in her actions and, on appeal to the Court of Session, her petition was granted and she began to practise in Glasgow in 1920. Later, in 1931, she founded the first female-run legal partnership in London. Unbelievably, though, it was only in 2020, a hundred years after Anderson qualified, that a top-tier London law firm announced its first female senior partner.[4]

The Bar is every bit as elitist and male-dominated as London's magic circle of top law firms. As mentioned in the Bridge Report, the Inns of Court – with their ancient squares and baronial dining halls – are reminiscent of some of the country's top public schools and universities. Incidentally, neither Oxford nor Cambridge Universities awarded degrees to women in 1919 when the Sex Disqualification (Removal) Act was introduced.

----

[4] Freshfields announced Georgia Dawson as the first woman to lead a magic circle firm in November 2020.

The first female barrister to practice was Helena Normanton, an ardent campaigner for women's rights who came from a very difficult background. She was born in the East End of London in 1882, and just four years later, after the birth of a sister, her father was found dead in a railway tunnel. Her parents had already separated, but subsequent to her ex-husband's death, Normanton's mother moved to Brighton where she ran a boarding house and brought up her children alone. After winning a scholarship to the esteemed York Place Science School, Normanton became a pupil teacher until she left in 1900 following her mother's death, and she became responsible for her younger sister.

This most remarkable woman then went on to gain a first class honours degree from the University of London, a Scottish Secondary Teachers' Diploma from Glasgow University (where she also lectured in history), as well as a diploma in the French language, literature and history from Dijon University. This was all *before* she first applied to become a student at Middle Temple in 1918 (and was refused despite lodging an appeal with the House of Lords). She reapplied successfully on the 24th of December 1919, within hours of the Sex Disqualification (Removal) Act coming into force.

Normanton then scored a remarkable number of legal 'firsts' after being among the first two women called to the Bar in 1922. This included being the first married woman in Britain to hold a passport in her maiden name, the first female counsel to lead in a case at the High Court, and the first woman to conduct a case in the United States. In 1948, she was the first woman to lead the prosecution in a murder trial in an English court and, a year later, became one of the first two women appointed as King's Counsel.

Throughout her adult life, Normanton wrote and spoke about feminist issues and published her book, 'Everyday Law for Women' in 1932. In it, she explains how she had wanted to be a lawyer since the age of 12 when she visited a solicitor's office with her mother, who was unable to understand the advice given. Normanton saw this situation as a form of sex discrimination and wanted to help all women gain access to the law which, at the time, was a profession only accessible to men. She wrote, 'I still do not like to see women getting the worst end of any deal for lack of a little elementary legal knowledge.'

Normanton died in 1957, and it wasn't until October 2021 that she was honoured with a blue plaque unveiled by Lady Hale, another barrister who broke down barriers for women in the legal profession. 'Helena Normanton was the pioneer of female barristers,' Hale said at the time. 'She had to overcome a great deal of prejudice and discrimination. A blue plaque is a fitting tribute to her courage and her example to women barristers everywhere.'[5]

Hale is another pioneer in the industry, although 60 years had passed after Normanton was appointed one of the first two female KCs before Hale became the first female justice of the Supreme Court with her appointment in 2009. The daughter of two head teachers who forged a career in academia before working full-time as a barrister, Hale subsequently became the first woman President of the Supreme Court in 2017. She was under no illusion about the discrimination many of us who don't fit the traditional description of a lawyer continue to face when trying to build a successful career in our chosen profession. During an interview to mark the centenary of the Sex Disqualification (Removal) Act of 1919, she argued that the 'white and male judiciary is from another planet' and needed to become more diverse for the public to have greater confidence in it. She called for more balanced gender representation and swifter

---

[5] The Guardian Newspaper, 21 October 2021

progress promoting those from minority ethnic backgrounds and those with 'less privileged lives'.[6]

Some years earlier, in 2011, Hale told the InterLaw Diversity Forum, 'I regard it as quite shocking that so many of my colleagues belong to the Garrick Club, but they don't see what all the fuss is about.' The Garrick Club is one of London's oldest clubs and remains as synonymous with success as it always has done. It boasts a membership of illustrious authors from Charles Dickens to AA Milne and Kingsley Amis, thespians such as John Gielgud, Stephen Fry and Damien Lewis, as well as broadcasters Melvyn Bragg, Jeremy Paxman and Sir Trevor McDonald. Of course, these are all very successful men, however Lady Hale was complaining more about its powerful members than its famous ones. She was referring to the Garrick's long association with the legal profession where, along with supreme judges, many senior lawyers are members. Women, however, are still barred from Garrick Club membership.

In 2020, more than 100 QCs called on Garrick members to vote for women to be admitted at its annual general meeting through a petition stating, 'It is well known that The Garrick is a forum where senior members of the legal profession socialise with each other. Men are afforded an opportunity through their membership to form connections with senior legal practitioners to support their professional aspirations. This is an opportunity expressly denied to women and contributes to the gross underrepresentation of women at the top of the legal profession.' The petition failed despite:

- Women accounting for more than 50% of the judiciary
- 60% of solicitors being women, with barely half that proportion ever being appointed as a partner[7]

---

[6] The Guardian Newspaper, 1 January 2019
[7] Solicitors Regulation Authority, 31 January 2022

whilst, in the top ten law firms, that figure reduces to less than 18%[8]

- 50% of pupillages go to women, and yet merely 16.8% make KC[9]
- Women represent just 27% of High Court Judges, 23% of Appeal Court Judges, and only 17% of Supreme Court Justices[10]

Along with overt discrimination, such as that practised by the Garrick Club, these anomalies are the result of a systemic bias that has long been accepted as the norm (in countless industries) where women struggle to be treated fairly. Following on from the Sex Discrimination Act 1975, the Equality Act 2010 gave men and women equal legal status with protection from discrimination, harassment, and victimisation for a variety of areas, including pregnancy and maternity. However, banning established business behaviours doesn't necessarily bring about the desired change. In 2017, further regulations were introduced requiring companies with more than 250 employees to publish the difference in average pay between men and women in their workforce each year. In 2021, according to the Office for National Statistics, full-time male employees were earning 15.5% more than their female co-workers.[11] This unequivocal evidence of how a business values its staff – based on gender – is stark, despite a tacit acknowledgement of some companies submitting questionable data.[12]

Gender pay gap information is particularly interesting when looking at the British legal profession's top 10% of earners. Overall, in 2021, the top men earned between £500k and

---

[8] PWC Lawfirms Survey, 2018
[9] Bar Standards Board, January 2021
[10] InterLaw Diversity Forum Research, 2021
[11] ONS, October 2022
[12] The Guardian Newspaper, April 2018

£600k on average, while the highest-paid women earned *less than half* at around £250k.[13]

While these figures may be an extreme example of a gender pay differential resulting from an established male hierarchy, we all know women and minority groups continue to face discrimination in workplaces everywhere. They are merely a reflection of the world we live in, where men have dominated for a very long time.

Anthropologists reckon men first gained the upper hand in most global societies when we stopped being hunter-gatherers to begin farming around 12,000 years ago. With a general superiority in physical strength, they took charge of food production, and patriarchy soon followed. Throughout the ensuing millennia, we all practised and then inherited beliefs around gender roles that are difficult to challenge.

While there were doubtlessly people over the ages who questioned the rationale behind men's absolute authority, it is generally accepted that the 18th-century writer and philosopher Mary Wollstonecraft was the first published author to promote equality for women. A 'poor gentlewoman' who lived an unorthodox life, taking lovers and only marrying in her late thirties, she was unusual in having been able to support herself through her writing. 'A Vindication for the Rights of Women', published in 1792, is generally accepted as the birth of feminism, although the word was only coined after her death in 1797.[14] Wollstonecraft died just 11 days after giving birth to her

---

[13] InterLaw Diversity Forum Research, 2021
[14] Charles Fourier, a French philosopher first wrote about 'féminisme' in1837.

daughter, Mary Shelley, another accomplished author who led an unusual life and who wrote 'Frankenstein'.

It was much, much later before any tangible change in women's rights reached the statute books. Legislation to address the problems women and others continue to experience in the workplace are ongoing and desperately needed. They are just the beginning, however. We will only be treated as equals when there is a change in mindset among our political, spiritual and business leaders. These – predominantly male – powerful individuals need to show everyone how to embrace the advantages that change will bring.

Men may be in charge, but women too have been brought up with strongly held beliefs about the roles that are better suited to them. This was evident at the school I attended that had been founded during the first wave of the women's movement for girls to gain a sound academic education. We were strongly encouraged to build meaningful careers... as long as they fitted in with the more important demands of being a wife and mother.

That was during the 1990s, when there was already an established legal framework for working women and, even today, it seems that girls' aspirations are much the same. They believe their working careers should be secondary to that of their male partners.[15] Why, nearly a century after the appeal court ruled against the Dorset schoolmistress wanting to work after marriage, does such ingrained prejudice remain? And, more importantly, how can it be addressed?

I knew I needed answers to these questions if I wanted to establish a different, truly meritocratic law firm. To find out more and hopefully gain an insight into the myriad of inequalities in the workplace, I began to read. Among other books about why women fail to thrive in the workplace, I

[15] UCL, October 2017

came across The Next Smart Step by Kelly Watson and Jodi Ecker Detjen; it introduced the concept of unconscious bias.

Unconscious bias is where our brains make instant decisions that are invisible to us and made without thinking. They are patterns of thought resulting from a lifetime of personal experience and education. Unconsciously, we perform countless evaluations each day, based on what makes us feel most settled and secure. Given that we are more comfortable in familiar situations and with people we know, we tend to repeat the behaviours and thought patterns to which we're most accustomed.

Unconscious bias is so obviously a natural human trait that I was surprised not to have come across it before. By storing away everything life has taught us to date – along with inherited 'knowledge' from our parents and their parents before them – we automatically make safe decisions. This makes good sense. After all, why take unnecessary risks?

However, the flip side to unconscious bias and avoiding the unknown means we steer clear of situations and people who are different. We are less willing to try something new or be open to innovation, or a new perspective.

When partners in law firms or leaders in any other business consider who is most suitable for promotion, this unconscious bias works against women and minority groups getting a fair chance. The white, middle-class male will feel more confident in promoting someone who looks and talks like him, and who has had a similar background, than someone with whom he has little in common and is less able to relate to. To me, this unintentional, systemic misogyny is probably the main reason why there are so few women at the top of law firms or other big businesses, despite the existence of anti-discrimination laws. Unless something is done to challenge the system, at the current rate of change, it is estimated another 170 years will need to pass before equity is achieved.[16]

The other side of such a paradigm is the assumption that only women can be effective caregivers. That men aren't interested and don't want to be involved in their children's daily lives. Instead, they are perceived as forever seeking career promotion and relish working long hours outside the home. Such broad statements are unfair on everyone. I'm sure I worked with male lawyers who were loud and proud in staying late at the office to work on a big project when they would have secretly loved to get away. They wish they could have made it to their child's sports day, or picked their toddler up from nursery and had a hug.

Unconscious bias is woven into all our lives, and we're so enmeshed within it that we don't even realise how detrimental it can be. Affecting far more than the jobs we choose, or the careers we can build, it alters the way people treat us and what we expect from others.

Just think about how long women had to put up with sexual harassment in the workplace before the #MeToo movement finally changed the common perception of 'acceptable behaviour'. Until then, unwanted predatory conduct from male colleagues was ignored because, 'He's just being a bloke' or 'Well, what do you expect if you wear a short skirt/smile like that/look like that?' Just because Harvey Weinstein and Fox News CEO Roger Ailes were high-profile bosses who demanded sexual favours in return for helping women's careers doesn't mean there weren't similarly-led male hierarchies in countless other industries that didn't make newspaper headlines.

'It was 1993 and my first day with the company,' Cathy, an older colleague, tells me. 'I was invited into my boss's office for him to explain what was expected of me, but he then went

---

[16] 'The Next Smart Step', Kelly Watson & Jodi Ecker Detjen, 2021

on to describe how my predecessor had managed to get a really good promotion with his assistance.' It soon became clear that quick promotion came about following long 'business lunches' in a nearby hotel bedroom. When Cathy made clear his suggestion wasn't something she was comfortable with, her boss said – in that case – she would quickly be moved sideways into a dead-end role. Straight out of college, new to the marketing industry, and until then delighted to have landed a position with an upmarket global brand, Cathy was stunned. True to his word, her boss, a guy more than twice her age with a young family tucked away in the home counties, soon replaced her. And Cathy lost what could have been a great start to a career.

That happened 30 years ago, but it reminded me of a conversation I overheard in the office as a junior solicitor. Like Cathy's boss, the lawyer would have been in his mid-forties, and he was explaining to a male colleague how, as he didn't find his wife sexually attractive when pregnant, he took on a mistress to satisfy his needs 'when she's so tired and tubby.' Given his seniority in the firm, I didn't confront him, but wish I had. 'Have you looked in the mirror recently?' I should have asked. 'Your wife's tired with a big belly because you impregnated her with your child. What excuse have you got? You fat twat.'

Women put up with unreasonable behaviour at work because we were brought up to expect it. The rules were embedded into a system that was designed and run by men, for men. Even the language we use to describe leadership qualities is dependent on whether we're describing a man or a woman. The same descriptive characteristic can be a positive for one gender while a negative for the other. Men may be 'strong, resilient and forward-thinking' while women are 'demanding, ruthless and pushy'.

Women are every bit as affected by the same bias and buy into the stereotypes that hold us back. We've been programmed over the centuries to believe our main responsibility is to keep everything running smoothly at home. Any career we choose should fit in with that premise. We're also the ones to take on the majority of voluntary work in our communities. This can be helping out at our children's schools, local charities or lending a hand to vulnerable family members, friends and neighbours. We may need to work full-time, but what we earn shouldn't be a priority. Instead, we need to be well organised to cheerfully *do it all*. And we mustn't forget that we need to look good at the same time.

Once the concept of unconscious bias is pointed out to people and accepted, steps can be taken to acknowledge how it affects decision-making and respond accordingly. However, nobody likes to think they are prejudiced or unfair. We are all reluctant to admit to being biased and genuinely believe our decisions are open-minded and have been properly thought through.

When business leaders are asked why so few women and minorities make it to the top, they respond with a gamut of explanations that have nothing to do with discrimination. 'Women don't apply for these roles' or 'Give it time and more women will have made it through the promotion pathway' being two such examples.

It is widely acknowledged that blue chip companies with more diverse boardrooms are the most successful in today's rapidly changing world. Diversity and inclusion are frequently mentioned as key objectives but unless the restrictions imposed by unconscious bias are addressed, these aims and the future success of businesses will be seriously hindered.

It is also acknowledged that the legal industry has lagged behind others in embracing the change necessary to succeed in the 21st century.[17] Despite the Legal Services Act of 2007 – designed to help liberate the market and allow alternative business structures – lawyers are particularly reluctant to change. Today's bright young hopefuls in top legal firms continue to closely resemble those who came before them; rather than looking at the long-term goals of the firm, senior partners still prioritise their end-of-year drawings over everything else. Surely such traits should be perceived as Dickensian and as out of touch with today's commercial needs as Uriah Heep's unctuously mercenary ambitions?

Reading as widely as possible to fathom how best to structure my own firm, I saw the straitjacket that John Blinkered and others like him had created for their businesses. He didn't seem able to acknowledge that if his partnership's future leadership pool is restricted to those with whom he feels comfortable (younger versions of himself), it will no longer be fit for purpose. By excluding women, involved parents, and increasing numbers of people like me who don't want to 'paint themselves grey' before starting each morning, Blinkered Brothers was excluding the majority of qualifying lawyers. This couldn't make good business sense. There had to be a better model of law firm, and that's what I proposed to create.

---

[17] Cambridge University Executive & Professional Education, June 2016

7. My Vision

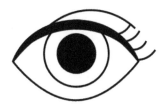

Stephenson Law came into being because I couldn't find a law firm I wanted to work for. I couldn't find a law firm that would enable me to bring my authentic, colourful self to work, tattoos and all. Looking around me, I saw a rapidly changing world that simply wasn't reflected anywhere in the sphere of my chosen career.

During an exciting period of digital innovation, most law firms still had very limited and outdated online identities; they had boring websites, minimal social media presence, and appeared to use computers as little more than clever typewriters or calculators. They continued to enjoy the clunky technology of early Star Trek while other industries adopted the sophistication of Avatar.

In addition to the technological ignorance, I was fed up with the traditional thinking, the prejudice, the discrimination, and the lack of tolerance for individuality and creativity.

My disillusionment with the industry was fully developed by the time I decided to leave Blinkered Brothers for the last time. That day was simply the moment I realised I would have to leave law altogether unless I did something to make a change. With Pete behind me, I already knew I wanted to run my own business and that moment of germination was when I knew *what* it would be. As my third child grew inside me, I was determined to work out how to build a business to fill the ever-growing gap between what law firms were offering and what was needed for the 21st century. A legal Pret A Manger for the business community – where clients are offered an accessible provision of good quality, reliable and transparently-priced advice to help sustain their companies.

It would be a new type of law firm, one that recognises we're all human beings with individuality, where clients are valued and lawyers are encouraged to be and give of themselves. I wanted to prove that a woman can have a successful legal career as well as enjoy her life as a wife and mother. I wanted to create something truly meritocratic, where every member of staff is respected for what they achieve, not what they look like, who they know, or what school they attended. Although I also wanted to earn a decent living, I could always do that working for someone else, so it was about much more than simply making money.

Of course, making money is necessary for any business to succeed, although I was fully aware that wanting to be profitable isn't something that would set my business apart from all the others out there. Even so, it was only later on that I discovered how important it was to have a strong purpose for starting my business. It became a reliable mantra, something familiar to fall back on when things got hard. When I lay awake at night worrying and asking myself why I started the firm in the first place, I'd remind myself of the goals I wanted to achieve, and that gave me the motivation to keep going.

I established Stephenson Law in 2017, ten years after the Legal Services Act of 2007 was passed and six years after it was implemented. The Act, after a decade of research, was designed to give consumers more choice in two distinct ways. Firstly, it allowed law firms to diversify into other professional services. Secondly, it allowed law firms to have 'alternative business structures' where they could be owned and managed by non-lawyers.

Until then, only lawyers were allowed to own firms that sold legal expertise. Consequently, they had complete control over how their knowledge was sold and how it was delivered. There could be no argument with the traditional legal partnership's billable hours system, where lawyers clocked the time spent on an account as they went along, and clients were landed with whatever fee that accumulated.

Understandably, this approach was (and still is) unpopular with clients who couldn't know the cost of a service in advance and budget for it accordingly. They basically had to share an 'open chequebook' and trust that the lawyer working for them wasn't particularly slow or dishonest about the hours recorded. With such a monopoly in place, and with no alternative available to clients, law firms paid scant attention to changes in the market or how other industries were evolving. They merely checked their hourly rates were in line with competing law firms to maintain the status quo.

As I'd discovered – while employed by Blinkered Brothers and KWS – a firm's talent pool had historically remained stable by picking out 'suitable' young associates willing to work long hours as the colourless cogs of a legal machine in the hope of one day becoming partner. Partners, enjoying the financial rewards of the billable hours system, rarely left the firm and saw no benefit in altering a model that had served them so well. Even after the introduction of the Legal Services Act, little accommodation, if any, was made for the changes it introduced.

The 2007 Act was a dramatic liberalisation of the industry. Yet, during my time as a freelance solicitor working for various firms in a multitude of business sectors, I'd witnessed no element of modernisation. Perhaps, more importantly, I saw no *desire* to change the archaic manner in which traditional legal partnerships continued to work.

I was determined that my new company would be in the vanguard of dragging the industry into the 21st century, and Stephenson Law would be founded on a different business model. One that would serve each and every stakeholder, whether owner, employee or client. Lawyers needed flexibility around when and where they worked, with defined aims and objectives, rather than merely clocking up billable hours in an office. Clients needed to know what they were purchasing and how much it would cost. I wanted to build rewarding relationships with an interest in, and understanding of, what clients were trying to achieve. As well as offering legal expertise, Stephenson Law would be an asset to their businesses, helping with critical analysis, negotiation, and creative problem-solving.

Law and creativity aren't words commonly seen in the same sentence because lawyers are typically seen as left-brainers… strong analytical thinkers focused on logic. Nevertheless, there's a lot of room for creative thinking whilst practising law and I was surprised that law firms placed no value on it, either during the recruitment process or appraisal of their lawyers. And yet, when seconded to clients, I found my creativity to be a highly valued asset.

When negotiating a client's needs, if I couldn't identify a creative solution, I was likely to be spending a lot of time going back and forth over the same points. Being able to 'think outside the box,' I was often able to help unlock sticky situations. Even when drafting contracts – where I had to adhere to restrictions and conventions – being creative helped properly reflect the client's requirements. On one occasion, I was brought in to a stalemate situation where, by merely reducing the duration of the contract's term, both parties were miraculously satisfied.

My services were in high demand throughout my time as a freelancer, and I was sure this was partly due to my ability and willingness to look at the 'broader picture'. I was determined that Stephenson Law would offer a holistic, long-term approach to its clients, based on mutual respect and benefit in the same way as it would with its lawyers.

In turn, after my personal difficulties in ensuring I could be a part of my children's lives as well as fulfilling my work commitments, I knew Stephenson Law would encourage an appropriate balance between work and family life for everyone who worked there.

While the landscape is starting to shift, few men are in a position to take up the caring reins as Pete did for me. Rightly or wrongly, it's still the case that mothers assume the majority of childcare responsibilities. This includes taking parental leave to look after a new baby, doing the drop-offs and pickups, or having to drop everything to collect a sick child from nursery. I know first-hand how female lawyers with children can be criticised for leaving work to pick up their children and are overlooked for promotion because of their childcare responsibilities. I also know first-hand how many excellent female lawyers are lost to the profession because of this inherent bias, never reaching the senior positions for which they are ideally suited.

Fran joined a top City firm after graduating with a first class honours degree in 2001. 'It was after the birth of my first child that I could see a change, a downgrade, in the type of project I was being given,' she says. 'I don't think anything I did would have changed the perception that my choice to become a parent effectively ended any career progression with that firm.'

After the birth of her second child, Fran moved elsewhere to a part-time role with an in-house legal team. 'I know I more than fulfilled everything demanded of me, and added a much-needed element of expertise, but never felt valued.' While Fran's husband, a lawyer who qualified at the same time as her, has now risen to partner in his firm, Fran has left the profession for a career in teaching.

The legal industry is losing lawyers like Fran despite studies showing how women possess impressive leadership skills that are often superior to men's, and that they generally have higher emotional intelligence and well-developed soft skills necessary for effective leadership. Women have also been shown to be more effective leaders than men in a crisis.[18]

I saw how being present in the office from early morning until late at night was a customary prerequisite for getting onto the promotional ladder in traditional partnerships. Law

---

[18] Harvard Business Review, June 2019

firms were littered with male lawyers bragging about the 'all-nighter' they just pulled or the 20 billable hours they worked yesterday. It demonstrated how the target-driven culture of billable hours caused lawyers to benchmark themselves against their colleagues and created constant pressure to keep up. And the partners loved it because the harder everyone worked, the higher their share of the profits would be.

This environment of valuing presenteeism and public displays of over-working only added to the disadvantage female lawyers already suffered through unconscious bias. Women are far less comfortable with self-promotion than men, and yet firms had no means of discerning the difference between confidence and competence. Little value was placed on the quality of work being produced or the presence of impressive leadership traits. Hence, confidence prevailed over competence, even where female lawyers met their targets and delivered excellent results.

Women weren't the only group of lawyers who – held back by the traditional partnership hierarchy – were undervalued and missed out on opportunities. As an article in the Financial Times reported in 2022, black lawyers and those from working-class backgrounds struggled to develop decent careers with well-established and prestigious law firms. Tom (not the same Tom I worked with at KWS), whose father was a builder, recalled how he proffered his birth certificate when he needed to formally confirm his identity on qualification. 'Haven't you come far…?' was the City firm's partner's mocking response. Aware his background would always be held against him in such an elitist environment, Tom moved into the public sector.[19]

Other working-class lawyers have spoken of being mocked for wearing brown shoes, having an accent that needed to be 'toned up', or attending a state school. 'I'm continually being

---

[19] Financial Times, 17 October 2022

asked where I'm from, despite both of my parents being born in the UK,' Lucy, a London-based black solicitor, told me.

Finally, there was the issue of looking right. For women, it was a question of needing to dress in the female equivalent of a man's suit, shirt and tie, while men had to wear the real thing. It seemed strange to me that items originally introduced during the Victorian era as casual outdoor garments for the upper classes had become both indoor clothing and a strict uniform for middle-class male office workers. Ties first came into use as neckerchiefs to keep a jacket or shirt closed at the neck and then became associated with being formally attired. Whatever its original use, the tie serves no practical purpose today, and whilst the office environment seems to have acknowledged this to some degree, it frustrates me that it still forms part of my boys' school uniform.

In the same way as I was unhappy with having to 'tone down' my personality when going to work each morning, I knew male lawyers who resented having to purchase a second wardrobe of clothes to achieve the same appearance of anonymity. They bought sombre-coloured suits that they would never have chosen to wear, merely to be accepted and taken seriously at work. How could being dressed in matching jackets and trousers, colourless shirts and ties have made them better lawyers? Surely they would have worked more happily and efficiently if they'd been able to wear clothes in which they felt relaxed and themselves?

A policy of wearing what matched your personality was adopted by Virgin Airlines in 2022, and the abandonment of gendered uniforms led to a 100% increase in job applications. All staff members are free to choose whether to wear skirts or trousers, tattoos no longer have to be hidden, and female crew members don't have to wear make-up. United, the US airline, made the same decision in June 2023 as well as introducing lapel badges displaying the employee's name and preferred pronoun.

To me, these were great moves by global brand leaders, and I hope they will be followed by others. Research has shown that people with tattoos are no less likely to be employed than those without inked adornment and that average earnings are the same for both groups. However, this doesn't reflect my experience in the legal profession and I know I'm not alone. For the record, my tattoos were chosen with great care, are a precious part of who I am, and I resented having to hide them when working for traditional law firms.

Despite the fact that around 30% of UK citizens aged 25-39 have tattoos,[20] it's not illegal for employers to discriminate against employees for having them. While attitudes are slowly changing, I spent years working in private practice being told to cover up the tattoos on my arm, and there is unquestionably a demographic that believes there is no place for them in the legal profession. Anyone with visible tattoos runs the risk of being stigmatised and studies have found women are judged more harshly than men. While I can categorically confirm that my tattoos don't affect my ability to practice law, this is not an opinion everyone shares. Apparently, as a tattooed woman, I am more likely to be judged as being promiscuous and a heavy drinker, as well as being less caring, intelligent or honest! Not exactly qualities sought after in lawyers.

It's commonly understood that first impressions are important, and our biases result in us making generalised judgements as to the character of someone based on their appearance alone. I've already discussed how being a woman or person of colour immediately affects the chances of career progression in the legal world, and being tattooed is another negative stereotype that causes unnecessary bias. People

---

[20] The Guardian Newspaper, October 2019

from diverse backgrounds and cultures with different perspectives can add tremendous value to a business and should be able to express themselves through their appearances.

The business case for inclusion and diversity is clear-cut, and while leading firms claim to promote these values, the evidence shows that they're not delivered. I was determined that Stephenson Law would encourage every member of the team to be their authentic selves at work and would offer a truly meritocratic environment for lawyers to demonstrate their capabilities and value to the business.

Another important element of my firm would be a holistic approach to staff development with the recognition that, despite our best efforts, we all have good and bad days. That, sometimes, we make mistakes.

Making mistakes when you're a lawyer can be catastrophic. As a junior lawyer, I would be told horror stories about multi-million-pound professional negligence claims and lawyers being struck off because they put a comma in the wrong place in a contract. The result was that I was terrified of making a mistake, despite it being an inevitable trait of being human.

During my training, I became accustomed to the barrier between me and clients; a barrier that was there to shield my firm from the risk of me doing anything negligent. Every sentence I wrote was checked at least once or, more likely, rewritten. Whilst a degree of comfort was taken from this very effective safety blanket wrapped around me, and I'm sure my skills improved, there was no acknowledgement that it also affected my confidence and self-esteem. Once qualified, and with this support largely removed, I felt extremely vulnerable and afraid of making a massive blunder that would come crashing down on me.

Fortunately, it never happened, although if it had, I would have hoped the Solicitors Regulatory Authority (SRA) would have understood the basic principle that 'mistakes happen' when determining disciplinary action. However, I've noticed an unfortunate string of decisions where junior lawyers have made bad decisions and been struck off as a result. This was despite evidence of poor leadership, toxic work environments and mental health issues.

'It may be that pressure of work or an aggressive, uncaring workplace could excuse carelessness by a solicitor or a lapse of concentration or making a mistake, but dishonesty of any kind is a completely different and more serious matter, involving conscious and deliberate wrongdoing.' This High Court judgement came about after the SRA wasn't happy when the Solicitors Disciplinary Tribunal (SDT) had suspended Sovani James, a junior solicitor, rather than have her struck off for an error of judgment. This was despite it being noted that James worked under such 'abominable stress' under an 'aggressive implementation of billing targets' that her hair had started to fall out.[21]

In my opinion, such draconian decisions only increase the likelihood of mistakes being concealed for fear of disproportionate sanctions. As a result, nothing is learned and a similar error is likely to re-occur in the future.

Instead, I believe that mistakes should be seen as an essential ingredient to turning junior lawyers into expert lawyers. In a profession with so much emphasis on continuous professional development, it's counter-productive to suppress them. When the time came for Stephenson Law to employ trainees and junior lawyers, I resolved they would have the freedom to make mistakes. Of course, such errors would need to be identified, openly discussed and fixed before work was shared with clients. This would be done in a culture where learning and development are the focus, and people are free to talk about the errors they make without judgment or blame. I also wanted a greater

---

[21] The Times Newspaper, 14 November 2018

recognition of the correlation between stress and fatigue and making mistakes. I strongly believe that a firm which succeeds in creating a culture where lawyers feel safe in making mistakes without fear of being shamed or punished will benefit from happier staff, better lawyers and, ironically, fewer mistakes.

Historically, the idea of keeping staff happy wasn't high on law firms' agendas because they had a monopoly both on legal services and training lawyers. There was such homogeneity within the industry that they didn't need to try. If a junior lawyer moved on, another would quickly be brought in, and partners almost never moved because of the power they wielded and the money they earned. Law firms had all the power in the client relationship and in the employer relationship, but as mentioned above, that changed following the 2007 Legal Services Act.

In other industries, it has long been recognised that a company retains its client base and its workforce only if they're happy. This may not have been a priority for other law firms, but would be of infinite importance to my company from the word go. Given the diverse pool of talent from which I was keen to recruit, I knew that Stephenson Law's most important asset would be its people. I wanted to make sure they felt valued and empowered as human beings as well as lawyers to challenge the status quo within the legal industry. I wanted a successful company that made money but got the balance right and valued its people.

At the same time, when I worked as a freelance solicitor, I was generally working as part of an in-house legal team where I often instructed other law firms on behalf of the client. Working as part of their legal team, I could see how unnecessarily hard it could be to get additional help. It opened my eyes to the client's perspective of the system. Whether we simply wanted some extra resource for a few days to make a deadline, or an expert opinion on a specific area of law, it felt like navigating a labyrinth. Even when there was a single straightforward question on a particular legal implication, the amount of to-ing and fro-ing demanded by the law firm seemed interminable and desperately complicated. I felt certain there had to be a smoother and simpler way for legal services to be delivered that could only make for a better and longer-lasting relationship between lawyer and client.

When considering how much demand there was for me as a freelancer, I was excited at the thought of what I could offer through my own company and with my own team. The contracts I'd been working on prohibited me from approaching any of the companies I'd worked with through other firms, but I knew there were plenty more. In a profession filled with so much possibility, it was frustrating to see it being held back by outdated practices, antiquated technologies, narrow-minded belief systems and prejudice.

I saw that the traditional partnership model created a short-term mindset with lawyers worrying about having enough work to enable them to meet their targets that day, week and month, with partners worrying about generating enough revenue to enable them to maximise their drawings that year. Little thought was given to the long-term, both in terms of investing in the business and its staff. My aim was for a firm that strives to be the best at what it does with a view to the future. Not the end of the year. Stephenson Law would be a successful long-term business.

With Pete beside me all the way, I'd finally found the confidence to give myself the creative freedom that so many of my colleagues lacked. It taught me to trust my ideas, push boundaries, and broaden the horizons of the industry. I had a clear concept of what I wanted to do, and there wasn't another lawyer I knew well enough (or trusted well enough) to share it with. Lots of people in my position would find a co-founder or investor, but I didn't want that. I didn't want my vision blurred by outside interference.

My initial purpose was to challenge the status quo that had been perpetuated – unchallenged and unchanged – within the legal industry since before women were permitted to practice. Ever since, I've been an outlaw on a mission to build a forward-thinking, innovative law firm which puts people at the heart of everything it does. Making law humane.

8. A Business Plan

My vision of Stephenson Law – and how it would provide a different approach to delivering legal services – was clear in my mind and made complete sense. It needed to offer a range of excellent services in a transparent and straightforward manner that demonstrated mutual respect to everyone involved. It would recognise that, whether client or lawyer, we are all human beings with unique qualities and differences. I wanted to create a truly meritocratic working environment that encouraged lawyers to give of their best and support clients with creative solutions absent from legal jargon. I knew it wouldn't be easy to achieve, yet I was certain it was achievable.

I had come across numerous stories from people who had wanted to start their own law firms. Many had met with insurmountable obstacles, the most notable being the cost of professional indemnity insurance.

'I'd need 10 Downing Street along with Buckingham Palace on my books just to cover the cost of PI insurance,' one property lawyer told me. Although I've since heard of insurers who simply refuse to cover firms specialising in conveyancing, I never figured out if any of these people actually tried to start their own law firms. Or if they just thought about it and the stories they were sharing with me prevented them from even taking their first steps!

The first thing I did was choose a business name. I wanted something that was personal to me as well as representative of its purpose. Stephenson Law was perfect.

Next, I needed a logo.

I've always loved animals, and while a lot of law firms and professional service companies use their name or initials to create a logo, others use an appropriate animal to help symbolise and promote the character of their business. A lion indicates strength, courage and authority, an owl is thought to be wise and dependable, whereas a butterfly suggests freedom and perfection. I wanted to infer all of those characteristics, and – discounting any animal that was already associated with an existing legal firm – I somehow came across the flamingo and couldn't let it go. I didn't know why it stuck in my head, although I now believe it was because flamingos are so distinctive, quirky and different. All characteristics with which I readily identify.

For a start, there's the amazing phrase about 'being a flamingo in a flock of pigeons'. It immediately says we can shine and stand out no matter where we are, where we are from, or what our differences are because we're proud of *who we are* and *what we do*. This straightforward message complemented the brand I was creating so boldly and yet equally succinctly. Stephenson Law – serene and graceful with a sense of purpose – would be a flamingo flying within a flock of pigeons (busy following one another to who knows where).

In turn, when we see a flock of pigeons arrive, it's often when they swoop down to poke and peck around morsels of food, scrapping and squabbling over breadcrumbs. I loved the idea of Stephenson Law having the elegance and panache of a flamingo – balanced high on one leg – while other firms are dull and dowdy pigeons scuffling around below.

Understanding how a strong online presence was vital for the type of forward-thinking business I wanted, I was keen for the logo to use visual imagery that immediately conveyed its character and difference. Unlike other law firms, Stephenson Law wouldn't be colourlessly marketing everything to everyone and making sure it offended nobody. Instead, it would stand proudly alone on its one-legged logo as brilliantly expert in just a few specialist areas.

An unintended advantage of choosing the flamingo as the logo was the countless variety of merchandise that was already out there! Whether you wanted a flamingo mug, notebook, candle, t-shirt, soft toy or pink grapefruit-flavoured gin, you could find one. On Amazon UK, you can browse among more than 3,000 flamingo products that have nothing to do with me or my company. And yet we benefit each time anyone associated with Stephenson Law sees anything with that unusual-looking bird… because they are reminded of us. And people frequently let us know. We've even had a client send a photo of their baby in a pink flamingo sleepsuit.

Choosing Stephenson Law's splendid logo was still months away when I had that seminal conversation with John Blinkered in May 2016. I needed to give birth and get the business up and running before it could start making money, so I took a short stint of maternity leave and continued to freelance until June 2017.

I spent countless hours trawling Google to find useful information about how to set up a law firm. Ultimately, there was very little available other than whatever was current on the Solicitors Regulation Authority (SRA) website. Nevertheless, that helped me understand what I needed to do to become authorised and what it meant to run a regulated law firm.

Initially, I had to work out whether there was a requirement for me to be authorised by the SRA. At the time, I remember thinking that I didn't want to restrict myself from providing certain types of legal advice, so being regulated seemed like the logical option. I also wanted to make sure there could be no misunderstanding about the gravitas of Stephenson Law, despite its mission to challenge tradition and embrace innovation. It still needed to stake its claim in the marketplace as a credible provider of legal services.

The next question was which type of authorisation to apply for, as there were three options:

- Licensed Body – an 'Alternative Business Structure', the industry definition of a law firm that is wholly or partially owned by non-lawyers and introduced following the Legal Services Act 2007

- Recognised Body – a legal firm wholly owned by lawyers
- Recognised Sole Practice – a legal firm owned by and run by a single solicitor

I decided to apply for authorisation as a Recognised Body because I intended to grow Stephenson Law and planned to take on additional owners at some point in the future. At the time, I didn't envisage branching out into non-legal services and could see that the application for a Licensed Body was also considerably more expensive and complicated. I already thought the amount of information required for registering a Recognised Body was vast and included a daunting number of accompanying forms to complete. It wasn't rocket science, though I'm not going to lie – it was a process that had definitely not been designed for the faint-hearted.

As always, Pete supported me through each step of the journey, which lasted pretty much as long as my pregnancy. He assured me we'd manage financially but, with a growing family to support, every penny counted. I needed to work out *how much* it would all cost. As I didn't initially intend to hold client money, my initial registration fee would be less than £500, which was affordable. However, another important element was insurance, and I knew that would be considerably higher.

As part of my application, I needed confirmation that an insurance company was prepared to insure me. The professional indemnity insurance would have to be in place before I could practise, which was a major worry as I understood it could be prohibitively expensive, assuming I could get it at all!

Once again, I was lucky to find an extremely friendly, helpful and patient insurance broker called Claire, who talked me through the whole process. She explained that for me to obtain an insurance quote, I had to submit another slightly different but still substantial pile of documents to those for the SRA. She also explained the 'run-off' insurance premium, which protects clients making a claim against a law firm that has closed down. It's a one-off payment, but at around 400% of the annual premium, it's an added incentive to make sure anyone starting out is fully committed.

Claire's help and experience were invaluable because she also pointed me in the right direction to find templates for creating a business plan. Along with financial projections, this was a major part of the SRA application and meant I needed to bring together the multitude of ideas in my head that were my vision for Stephenson Law.

I had to really drill down into the detail of what my business was going to look like. What were the services I was going to provide? How was I going to be different from my competitors? Who were going to be my clients? How was I going to persuade them to use Stephenson Law? What would it look like in three years? Who would be working alongside me? What would be its turnover? How much money would it make?

It was like being on an episode of Dragon's Den. Except, of course, I was pitching my business to the SRA rather than three or four millionaire entrepreneurs sitting on comfy armchairs in a TV studio. And while I was confident I could offer a more personable and humane legal provision in commercial law than traditional firms, I still wasn't sure how I would win clients or what my turnover would be.

Nevertheless, the questions needed to be answered within a reasoned business plan that defined which areas of legal expertise Stephenson Law would deliver, how it would generate value, and how it would convert that value into profit. With that in mind, I had to reflect on what I thought my clients would want, how they would want it delivered, and how I could best meet those expectations. Apart from any SRA requirement, this is extremely important for *any* new business to consider, given the estimation that 42% of startup businesses fail because there is no market need for their services or products.[22]

To get started, I prepared a comprehensive description of all the different aspects planned for Stephenson Law, as well as a three-year projected profit and loss statement. I included any supporting evidence I could find to help me articulate the logic behind founding Stephenson Law and why a new approach to delivering legal expertise to the corporate world was needed and would be welcomed. This extended across the organisational and financial architecture of the business, alongside costs, revenue, client behaviours and competitor movements. The profit and loss and cash flow statements were simply what I believed would be the value of sales on a monthly basis minus costs, and the lead time of when I expected clients to pay my invoices.

As can be appreciated, this level of insight took time that wasn't easily available while freelancing, although I thought of little else during my evenings and weekends. Once on maternity leave, I started to collate everything, ready to put the SRA application together and checked I'd left nothing out. I made very clear my willingness to take on the obligations I'd be assuming in owning a law firm and how confident I felt about what I was undertaking.

Assuming I'd be working alone initially, I described the areas of legal expertise with which I was most familiar and planned to offer potential commercial clients. These were mainly services in contracting and technology that I knew were in demand (out of necessity) by in-house legal teams. Significantly, I didn't expect this to be deemed high-risk work, and hoped this would improve my chances of obtaining an insurance quote. Having been told that only 25% of applications were being offered insurance terms at the time, there was no room for error in this detailed

---

[22] Engenersis, May 2022

explanation. I illustrated how I would provide services in the client's office or a small office I planned to rent in central Bristol.

When it came to turnover, I assessed how much Blinkered Brothers and others charged their clients for my time. It was double my freelance rate, so I calculated a daily rate I felt to be reasonable and multiplied that by the average length of contract I'd previously worked on.

The degree to which my estimations of how the business would develop ('guesstimations') was frightening; it made me worry about what could happen if I was completely wrong. Two years down the line, could the SRA pull me up on making false claims? Fortunately, Claire was close at hand to assure me that the business plan only needed to make realistic projections and that I wasn't expected to make any guarantees. What mattered was that my strategy was achievable, well thought-out, and gave the insurers and the SRA no cause for concern. Interestingly (and something Claire told me to take into consideration), any revenue forecast I made would be taken into account when calculating my insurance premium. Consequently, I wasn't tempted to be overly optimistic.

Another critical element of my business plan was to demonstrate how Stephenson Law would comply with the SRA Code of Conduct. Although this was an area covered during my legal training, I needed a much deeper understanding of it, as well as the roles and responsibilities involved in being the owner of a law firm. I would be both the Compliance Officer for Legal Practice (COLP) and Compliance Officer for Finance and Administration (COFA) for Stephenson Law.

Fortunately, I found some really helpful compliance guidance at The Law Society and also took up a subscription with an online legal management and compliance platform, which gave me access to support and various template policies.

Finally, I felt I'd got my head around it all. However, before applying to the SRA, I submitted my business plan as part of my application for professional indemnity insurance. I waited with bated breath in the knowledge that without insurance, there was no way to take things further with the SRA. It was a crucial wait and my options were limited as there aren't many insurers willing to back startup law firms.

If someone was willing to insure me, I'd need to be able to pay whatever premium they asked for. Pete and I had discussed what we could afford and knew our meagre savings wouldn't be enough. As a result, Claire put me in touch with a finance company that dealt in legal insurance and when I received an insurance quote for a little over £5k for the first year, I was delighted when they agreed to make the loan. I also knew that if an insurance company thought my business plan was up to scratch and a finance company was willing to back me, I was in with a good chance that the SRA would, too. With my insurance quote in hand, I sent off my application for authorisation to the SRA. Their website told me it would take three months to hear back.

I was finally coming to the end of my contract with Blinkered Brothers and looked forward to taking a break with baby Bertie and the rest of the family before jump-starting Stephenson Law. Until I had authorisation, I knew I couldn't do any more. Then, within a couple of weeks of making the application, someone contacted me with a few queries about the business plan. They were direct questions that I was able to answer on the phone, and the guy told me I'd hear back in due course. As a result, I anticipated having to wait another couple of months, but just a fortnight later, the authorisation arrived. The flamingo had hatched. Stephenson Law could be launched.

Describing the various hurdles involved in setting up a new law firm makes it appear quite simple when it was anything but. Rather than a hundred-metre sprint where you can see the finish line from the word go, it was like following the unmarked track of a never-ending marathon, in concrete trainers, where reaching the finish line was an impossible dream. The whole journey was so tortuous to navigate that, once I'd become established, I was keen to help others avoid the pitfalls and obstacles I encountered on the way. By the time Stephenson Law was ready to be launched, I fully understood why so many before me had given up on trying to found their own firms, and how this could only be a negative thing for the legal profession.

In 2017, I was one of more than 620,000 businesses that were launched in the UK. Despite that being an impressive figure, it should be noted that over 450,000 businesses were dissolved in the same period. It is incredibly difficult to get any small business off the ground and comfortably afloat, with an estimated 20% failing in the first year and that figure increasing to 60% in the following two years.[23] So, while I was delighted that Stephenson Law had made it to the starting grid, it was hardly in pole position with just me in the driver's seat. I still look back at that time and wonder at my audacity – and my naivety. I had little idea of what it would take to make sure Stephenson Law was in the 40% of small startup businesses that reached their fourth year of trading.

---

[23] The Daily Telegraph Newspaper, May 2019

I've since discovered that for businesses that go the distance, data overwhelmingly points towards one thing: an intimate understanding of the unique value the business provides to its customers.

Rather than scribbling sparks of genius onto paper napkins, successful entrepreneurs set foundations with a considered business proposal. In order to persuade an insurance firm I was worth the gamble and gain SRA authorisation, I had to frame a well-drafted plan to demonstrate a deep understanding of my chosen market and the business model I'd chosen to deliver a valued service to my potential clients.

I'd taken a long time to formulate a realistic blueprint for Stephenson Law and even longer to ensure that it was concise, appealing and effective. It had been fundamental in winning the confidence of insurers and the SRA to enable me to start my own law firm.

I'm sure there have been many great businesses that were formed from a stroke of genius, but I'm equally sure many others have weathered the ages with iron-clad business plans to show they were firms with proven purpose.

9. The First Year

When I received the approval from the SRA, it felt unreal. After years of being dissatisfied, certain there was a better way to deliver legal services, and then months of working through reams of paperwork, I'd done it. I'd jumped through all the hoops and set up my own firm. I was finally able to challenge the system!

Instead of the three-month wait I'd expected, it had taken just a few weeks, and once the insurance was in place, there was nothing to hold me back. The timing was so neat that I finished the Blinkered Brothers contract on a Friday and started working for Stephenson Law on the Monday.

'Why not take a break?' Pete asked when the SRA authorisation came through so quickly. He knew I'd been looking forward to some time at home with Bertie. 'Would a fortnight off make that much of a difference? Wouldn't it be worthwhile for you to take a bit of a holiday first?'

'I just can't,' I told him. It was as if everything I'd done since first deciding to go into law had led me here. It had taken so long and been such an effort that I couldn't wait any longer.

Pete shrugged his shoulders. 'If that's what you want… In any case, I know you'll be brilliant.' He smiled and put his arms out for a hug.

Despite my situation being exactly what I wanted, I was simultaneously excited and scared. It was like skydiving from 10,000 feet and loving every moment of the freefall's exhilarating terror while anxiously waiting to pull the ripcord for the security of the open parachute. The success of Stephenson Law no longer depended on obtaining insurance cover or SRA authority. I couldn't blame any failure on something or someone else. It only depended on me persuading other businesses that I was the best lawyer to deliver their legal requirements.

Until the SRA approval had come through, allowing Stephenson Law to trade, I'd been unable to do any marketing or even publish my website. Everything had to be completely ethical and within the regulatory constraints. As a regulated law firm, there was a specific day on which I could start trading. If I'd approached clients earlier, or if anybody had contacted me for professional advice, I wouldn't have been able to help as I wasn't insured or registered. So, on that first Monday morning of official existence, when my tiny flamingo was a mere hatchling in an enormous flock of pigeons, my first job was to win clients.

I probably sent out 150 messages over the first two days. Through LinkedIn or direct email, I approached everyone I'd ever worked with, known through law school or any professional capacity, and let them know I'd set up my own company. I pointed them to the flamingo logo of my rudimentary, colourful and informative website to find out more. Knowing I'd need to widen my network, I asked for any introductions they felt could be useful. I went into overdrive to find any work I could because I didn't have a single lead. I hadn't been in private practice long enough to build up a client following, and I had no sales experience.

It didn't take long to receive my first response and a request for further details about what services I could provide. It was a pivotal moment. I held my breath as I replied in what I hoped was a calm and professional manner to suggest an initial meeting. Within just a few days, more people came back to me asking for more information, some putting me in touch with others who needed my help. Before I knew it, work was coming in, and what started as a trickle soon became a torrent. I was ecstatic. My little bird was already lifting its graceful neck and stretching its wings.

Suddenly, from having no clients at all, I realised I wasn't going to manage alone. I needed another lawyer quickly to help me cope with the demand. Fortunately, one of the people I'd contacted was Corrine, a friend from law school who told me she was looking for some short-term, contract freelance work. When I got back to her a second time, with an altogether different request, she readily agreed to come and lend a hand for a couple of months.

Once the ball was rolling, I didn't want to lose momentum and began to consider where and what my target market was. Initially, I looked for local businesses through Google, trying to find out who was leading the legal teams and if anyone I knew could help me get in touch with them. Otherwise, I'd go in cold and drop them an email or a LinkedIn connection request.

Having discovered the value of social media and particularly LinkedIn, I regularly updated my profiles on several platforms to ensure any potential client knew my values and what I was trying to do. I recognised that Stephenson Law – an unknown new firm – would mean nothing to the people I approached. The reality was that I was promoting myself and what I could offer them. Being a good lawyer is much more than knowing the law so, confident in my ability and track record, I did my utmost to convince potential clients that I could provide what they needed.

I always made clear that it was all about what I could do *for them* and help their businesses rather than promote my own. I also did my homework researching both their businesses and their industries, as well as the areas in which I thought I could be of help. The messages needed to strike the right balance between giving people enough information (so that they'd want to meet me) but not too much where I came across as pushy. The end of the message always had a call to action with a suggestion of meeting up for coffee or a chat.

At the same time, right from the beginning, I wanted clients to know that Stephenson Law was different, and very soon after its launch, I made my first LinkedIn post about tattoos. It started with 'Let's talk about tattoos' and included a photo of me and my ink. That was one of the few times I've done something when Pete advised against it. I was super nervous but went ahead and posted it anyway, and was overwhelmed by the positive response. It was apparent that lots of people agreed with me that tattoos shouldn't be stigmatised in professional settings, and I received dozens of messages from people with their own stories of how their tattoos were perceived in their workplaces, which was mostly negative.

In that first month, I'd be so pleased when someone agreed to meet me for the first time to discuss their needs and while nervous, would make certain I'd found out as much as I could about them beforehand. During the meeting, I would do much more listening than talking; my help would stem from fully understanding the problems they were facing. I would ask lots of questions about them, their business, their challenges, and short- and long-term goals. Only after paying proper attention could I seriously respond with ways I thought I could help. It was an exciting time and although high pressure, I'm sure my enthusiasm came across in a positive way.

Corrine was a lifesaver. She had an amazing 'can do' attitude to everything that came our way... 'I'll deal with this', 'Let me get back to them on that.' And, between us, we did whatever it took to ensure Stephenson Law delivered its promise.

I've had so many 'first meetings' since those early days, and while I know that no two are ever the same, the one key constant is being able to listen attentively and react accordingly. The difficulty of knowing a law firm's costs in advance was a common complaint, and I did my very best to design a retainer service that gave as much cost certainty as possible. While this was based on time, given my level of client retention, my strategy of complete transparency and 'no surprise invoices' evidently worked. I soon learned that building a rapport with the person was the most important part of an initial meeting. Although a successful business may be one that can show a profit on a regular basis, it is still owned, run and managed by human beings. This obvious fact of life is something I still feel most law firms overlook to their detriment.

In any case, my belief that there was a demand for a law firm that offered a more personalised approach, one that was proud to show it had character and humanity, started to prove itself. In my first month of trading, I turned over £17,000 and knew I was on my way.

As a startup firm, I wasn't approaching Coca-Cola or Facebook, although I was still ambitious with the companies I contacted. One of my very first clients was a major shoe retailer and regional employer. I had no pre-existing relationship with them and had simply emailed their Chief Legal Officer to introduce myself and ask for a meeting. 'I don't think I've ever worked with a pink-haired lawyer before,' he told me when we met. 'And certainly not one with such decorated arms.' It was a warm day, so I'd worn a sleeveless dress rather than the androgynously boring uniform of most lawyers. That first summer, I got a couple of other big contracts because in-house legal teams needed extra support over the holiday period. We were pretty busy, and knowing Corrine had plans to go elsewhere in the early autumn, it was evident I needed to bring in more help. I decided to search for another qualified lawyer as well as someone more junior to join us.

Stephenson Law had been set up as a limited company, and I was already on its payroll while Corrine invoiced as a consultant solicitor. With an accountant looking after the bookkeeping, it was time to take on other PAYE members of staff, and I soon found a brilliant law graduate.

Anna joined us at the little, serviced office in Park Street, central Bristol, that I'd rented. There was always flexibility in the way we worked, but at the very beginning I wanted her to come in every day. Still needing to do her LPC, Anna began as a paralegal and a little later became the company's first trainee solicitor. Before long, Corrine had moved on and it was just Anna and me based in Park Street. We made a great team, and I decided it was time for some professional photos for the website.

'You've got a great smile,' said the photographer as Anna posed for her picture. 'Maybe lift your collar a little?' Anna did as she was told and lifted the collar on her blouse before smiling again. I then realised that lifting the collar on her blouse covered a tattoo that had previously been visible. At first, I didn't react – after all, it was standard practice for any law firm's headshots to be blandly acceptable. Quite quickly, however, I felt an overwhelming sense of discomfort; it didn't feel right that she was being asked to cover a completely inoffensive tattoo.

'Sorry, no,' I said. 'I'd like the tattoo to show. It's an important part of Anna.'

The refreshed website was a success and – missing Corrine from the moment she left – we were desperate for another qualified solicitor to join us. This proved to be an increasingly difficult problem as time went on and work continued to flow in.

My original approach to garnering business had been a success, and after a promising first month and the updated website, it didn't slow down, with plenty of new opportunities arising. However, being so concerned about attracting new clients, I hadn't stopped to consider whether there were obstacles that prevented me from attracting suitable lawyers. At the same time, I was confident there were plenty out there who, like me, weren't happy with their jobs in traditional firms. I always remembered one colleague at KWS saying, 'You're not supposed to enjoy your job, Alice. That's why you get paid to come in each day.'

A few years down the line and I was even more convinced that he was wrong. Any good lawyer should be able to find their job fulfilling, as well as enjoyable and well-paid. My problem was how to convince one that Stephenson Law – a new company with precisely one qualified solicitor – was where they could find that satisfaction. Lawyers are naturally risk-averse, so why hadn't I thought of this before? Why would any solicitor want to come and work for a company they've never heard of?

With just me and Anna for quite a long time, it was really hard. Her efforts were invaluable, and she was doing a tremendous amount to support me, but I still had to do the majority of the legal work. In addition, I had to maintain the momentum with the marketing, keep on top of compliance, and manage everything else involved in running a business.

As well as needing a fully qualified lawyer, we needed to find a good one! There was no point in employing someone who failed to understand what I was trying to achieve. I wanted someone with similar values and the ability to see a better future with a firm offering a different perspective. So, once again, I used LinkedIn and started to headhunt solicitors with profiles I thought looked like a good fit. I'd send messages along the lines of, 'Would you like to come and work with me in this amazing new business I've set up to change the legal world?'

Understandably, most people probably thought I was a complete nutter and ignored me. Eventually, though, Susie replied and could see exactly what I was attempting to do. Again, it was a pivotal moment. So exciting. And such a relief.

Since winning the firm's first contract, I'd worked at a ridiculous rate to keep on top of everything through a roller-coaster of almost a year. To say I was burning the candle at both ends was an understatement – there almost was no candle. Night after night, I'd be finishing emails propped up in bed into the early hours with Pete sound asleep beside me. And after barely enough time for a decent snooze, I'd be standing under a hot shower trying to wake up again, while he and the children were still in the land of nod. I was always aware, however, that (at least) I was slogging away on my own terms. Plus, we hadn't spent the year lining the pockets of some senior partner who didn't even know who we were. Even so, it was a wonderful feeling to know the legal workload would be shared.

Soon, I hired Susie, a lawyer who had just qualified from a highly reputable firm, but I now wanted to find someone to help run the business side of things. I needed an experienced practice manager, someone I could rely on while I concentrated on growing the company.

Once I found Nina, who became our fourth employee, I was able to take a breath, and for the first time since starting the business, Pete and I took the children away for a weekend. I even felt relaxed enough to leave my laptop at home.

As a regulated law firm, there were office procedures that needed to be closely monitored. Nina, with a lot of legal admin experience, took on much of that responsibility and was soon an invaluable member of the team. As well as helping me with the onboarding of clients and invoicing, she also took on much of the compliance paperwork, which was important to stay on top of. This included issues like checking a new client wouldn't create a conflict of interest for the firm with an existing client, and making sure our finances were always compliant with the SRA account rules.

During the first couple of years, we were charging clients at a day rate in the same way as if they were employing a freelance solicitor. My pitch argued we were a better alternative to an individual consultant as we were offering consultancy services as a team – albeit a team of three and, as mentioned above, I made sure our estimations for a project were detailed and accurate. For me, it was a win-win because I was doing the same work as I'd always done, and the client was paying the same as if they'd gone through Blinkered Brothers or some other firm for my services. The only difference was that 100% of the fee they paid came into my firm rather than a substantial amount of it being creamed off by another company. This system wasn't one I wanted to maintain in the long term, but it served me and my clients well until I found something better.

It was now late 2018, and during those first 18 months, every decision I'd taken to establish the firm and help make it succeed was based on what I could glean from the internet and discuss with Pete. There was no point of reference offered by the SRA or the Law Society with advice for new legal firms. That all changed when we got accepted onto a scheme funded by NatWest Bank to help young businesses grow.

The NatWest Accelerator programme offered wraparound support to assist UK entrepreneurs in scaling up to the next level. It included free open office space, where we were mentored along with lots of other young, ambitious companies, many of which were in the tech industry. We were offered a mix of one-to-one coaching on different aspects of running a business as well as talks and discussions on topics like leadership development and diversification.

It was an invaluable experience, and as the only law firm on the scheme, it enabled us all to network and get to know other people running a whole variety of organisations. They would come to us for legal advice, and until then, having generally worked for quite large companies, I'd never considered the startup market. Although we were in different industries, I discovered a lot of them were facing similar dilemmas to ourselves. Whether it was worrying about where we'd be this time next year, cash flow issues around how to encourage clients to pay promptly, or the most successful way to build a cohesive team, we learned a lot from one another. Working side by side with other businesses made me realise how hard it is for startups to get legal support and how intimidating it can be, as well as super expensive.

As a result, we started working a lot more with startups, but soon realised they didn't have a lot of money(!), which made it hard to make the books balance. It was a market we returned to later, but at that time, our attention favoured working with scaleups.

These were generally tech companies that, having secured some funding, had survived the initial startup phase and were on a trajectory for growth. It was a business area I found fascinating and was rapidly expanding with a speed of development that was quite mind-boggling. They covered a gamut of disciplines, such as EdTechs building platforms for schools, colleges and universities, or HealthTech for hospitals where the growth of AI was palpable. One of our clients was developing a women's urinal to overcome the inevitable queues at festivals and other popular events. For such an age-old problem as inadequate female toilets, why hadn't anyone thought of this before? I loved the possibility of helping cutting-edge businesses establish a legal framework in which they could take their ideas and dreams forward.

Discovering this area was a stroke of luck and was when I first felt comfortable about defining a target market. Rather than work with any company or business sector, it felt like Stephenson Law had found its natural home in the early-stage tech industry. Like us, these scaleups were innovators challenging the status quo. They were taking a different perspective on traditional practices across society with ground-breaking technology. It had to be the perfect place for my fledgling flamingo to thrive among others looking for change. For the time being, at least, this was where I wanted the business to grow.

10. Sell, Sell, Sell

The Oxford English Dictionary defines a business as 'The activity of making, buying, selling or supplying goods or services for money'.[24] The Cambridge University Press describes it a little more succinctly as 'The activity of buying and selling goods and services'.[25]

In other words, there has to be an element of buying and selling for any business to operate. Businesses can take many forms, but as a general rule, they offer a product or service that another party is willing to purchase. That's how I've built my business. A law firm that earned £17k in its first month and – after targeting a suitable market – over £1m in its second year.

Running a law firm is like running any other business, and to achieve success needs to:

- sell its services to new and existing customers
- sell its competence and business plan to the SRA, insurers, investors and lenders
- sell its credibility to strategic partners and suppliers
- sell its vision to prospective and existing employees

Somehow, perhaps because law is a profession rather than a trade, the idea that it's a business is often overlooked and almost frowned upon. I've never understood this snobbery and am proud to have created an entity that offers others employment and an excellent level of service to clients. What is there to be ashamed of?

When I was a solicitor working for other law firms, 'selling' had no place in my professional life. Even today, the 'S' word doesn't exist in the majority of legal practices. Instead, discussions centre around 'BD' or Business Development without defining exactly what it entails. There's a lot of talk about 'networking' and 'pursuing strategic opportunities'

---

[24] OED
[25] CUP

without anyone actually having the chance to learn the skills necessary to achieve any of it. Despite sales being fundamental to a law firm's success, the concept of 'selling' remains pretty alien.

Shortly after starting Stephenson Law, I realised that my ability to sell was going to make the difference between its success and failure. My ability to 'win clients' was merely a euphemism for my ability to 'sell to clients'. Until then, I hadn't known that I could sell – after all, I'd never had any sales training – or even realised that I was selling. But I've since realised that successful businesspeople and entrepreneurs spend most of their time selling. And selling effectively.

Effective selling is being able to lead a person or group of people to make a decision for a mutually beneficial transaction. To achieve this, a good salesperson has to be a persuasive communicator who interacts successfully with others through listening and empathising to help solve a problem and reach an agreed goal. At the same time, there's more than a smidgen of truth in the saying, 'If you pretend that everyone you meet has 'Make me Feel Important' written on their forehead, not only will you be successful in sales, you will be successful in life'. Nevertheless, selling covers three primary categories that are appropriate, depending on the type of client or other party involved in the sale.

The most straightforward is Product Selling, where a salesperson promotes the advantages and features of a specific product or service. In this situation, questions from potential clients can be largely predictable. The product or service may be treated in a similar way by a wide range of different users, and as long as the seller has properly researched the client's business needs, any queries should be easily satisfied. However, the seller has to remember that a prospective client is valuable and fragile and, like any perishable item, needs to be treated with care. I had to bear this in mind during a meeting when, after having made my pitch, I was being asked increasingly personal questions such as 'Do you enjoy your work?', 'Are you married?', 'How do you cope with your work-life balance?' And when he asked, 'What would you struggle with the most?', I responded light-heartedly with 'Resisting dark chocolate.' We both laughed, and I managed to steer the conversation back to business.

The next category is Solution Selling, where rather than being focused on promoting the virtues of what is being sold, the salesperson concentrates on how a client's problem can be solved. In this case, queries from potential clients can be more unpredictable, so the seller may turn the table to become the questioner through 'SPIN'. Initially, there need to be **S**ituational questions to find out about the current situation of a client's business with follow-up **P**roblem questions to identify the challenge that needs to be solved. Then comes the **I**mplication questions to understand the consequences of the problem and how this affects the client or his business. Finally, the **N**eed questions are used to evaluate the outcome of finding a solution through the purchase of the seller's product or service.

The third category is Insight Selling, where the challenge needing to be resolved is not initially recognisable to either the salesperson or the client. The problem has to be identified by both parties working together, where the seller acts as a business consultant discussing strategies and potential opportunities. They analyse how the seller's product or service – being bought and implemented – can facilitate the other party's goal. This could be helping a client's company follow a successful trajectory or simply closing a legal loophole in its terms and conditions.

I'd never heard about sales categories or SPIN when I founded a business to sell legal services. Nonetheless, I instinctively knew there was no 'one size fits all' in approaching prospective clients, and sometimes it was no more than recognising when it's a good time to simply 'shut up and listen'. In any case, it's much more a sense of collaboration than anything remotely coercive.

I'd always associated the word 'sales' with the stereotypical used-car salesman or market trader. The sort of dodgy dealer whose aim is to fool anyone they can find into buying something they don't need and which probably doesn't work. While, of course, there are individuals who knowingly pressure and cajole with empty promises to sell an inappropriate or poor-quality product, they are con artists and liars rather than salespeople. Instead, selling is explaining the logic and benefits of a decision in a persuasive manner. It isn't unpleasant or about forcing someone to purchase something they don't want or require. It's essentially a communication skill used by one person to demonstrate to another how a problem can be solved. Like many other skills, it can be learned through formal tuition or trial and error. In either case, to be good at selling requires confidence and resilience.

When I founded Stephenson Law, I already recognised the quality and value of my legal expertise as well as the manner of its delivery. As a result, I was confident in the product I was selling. This didn't mean I was an authority in every area of law, and would never suggest I was. However, if I could see that my own area of expertise could assist with a client's aims, I was more than ready to explain how I was almost certainly going to be the best person for the job. Firstly, though, I had to ensure they knew who I was and make myself visible to them.

Networking or getting to know people and being sociable with new acquaintances is a parallel skill to selling and of immense value. It is one I learned without even acknowledging it during my years of freelancing.

Working as a consultant solicitor, assignments appearing from nowhere – like the very first one I had when my old colleague Tim phoned me from Blinkered Brothers – were pretty hard to come by. Mostly, businesses simply approached a dependable law firm to find a suitable solicitor for a specific project. If the firm didn't have an appropriate in-house lawyer available or qualified to do the work, they would either list it with a freelance legal agency or get in touch directly with someone they already knew. After that initial freelance placement, I soon realised that the only way I would get work was by constantly staying at the front of the minds of the people making the decisions. When a new assignment came up, they needed to decide who to approach with the work. Someone they were confident could do it well and to the client's satisfaction. No matter how many pools of consultants I was registered with, there wouldn't have been much work if I hadn't made sure that people recognised I was there, I was good, and I was reliable.

I also knew that by the time I established Stephenson Law, it had gotten to the point where companies would ask for me personally through the agencies I was registered with. When I went on maternity leave with Bertie, a replacement was sent in who (in the client's opinion) didn't make the grade. Instead, the client asked for me to go back, as soon as I could, to finish the project. This, of course, gave me more confidence that my own law firm would be successful. Pete would joke that I talked like someone who'd already won the lottery before finding the time to buy a ticket.

I had effectively become good at selling myself without realising that's what I was doing. In my mind, I was simply building relationships with the people who were making decisions, which was necessary if I wanted to maintain a regular income. I'd also discovered that once a successful relationship had been created, it was important to maintain it for the possibility of future opportunities.

I now know that I'm a natural networker with the ability to interact comfortably with people from all walks of life. I love exchanging ideas with others and seeing if things can be done in a better, more efficient, or easier manner, and I find most people interesting when discussing something that's important to them. These were all aspects of selling and personal characteristics I've since been able to apply to my own business. And they made a real difference. Being able to easily sell a great product through effective communication was an invaluable tool for attracting and building relationships with clients. I only wish it could have been as successful when trying to convince lawyers to come and work with me.

Winning work for Stephenson Law was never the problem. My hardest sell was to staff. I really struggled to sell my vision to other lawyers.

In the early days, when it was just me sending my begging messages via LinkedIn, I was barely aware of what I was doing. And yet, in the same way as I was reaching out to contact potential clients, I was trying to contact lawyers using the same methods. Trying to persuade them to meet me. That was always the first very important step because if I could motivate somebody to sit in front of me and talk, my chances of success would be much higher.

Subsequently, what I think finally convinced other qualified solicitors to come and meet me was that most of them hated their jobs. They wanted to believe there was a better way for them to be lawyers. A different way from the traditional method of doing piecework for senior partners to fund their lavish holidays. Like me, they were sick of a system that expected them to turn into automatons each morning rather than be themselves. At the same time, it was a system they knew and trusted. Even if the treadmill that awaited them in the office tomorrow or next week would be equally tedious as yesterday and today, at least they were confident it would still be there for them to step onto. They felt secure in their jobs. I needed to offer more than a competitive salary to persuade them to leave the safety of their monotony.

When I had that first positive LinkedIn reply from Charlotte, who later chose to join us, I prepared myself just as thoroughly for our first meeting as if she were a potentially high-value account.

Neither Charlotte nor I may have described that interview as a sales meeting, but that's what it was. And it covered all three categories of selling. I eagerly promoted the advantages of coming to work for my company – the product I was selling. I ardently believed that choosing to work in an environment where Charlotte felt valued and could be herself would solve her dissatisfaction with her current professional role. The insight selling was in discussing how we could create a better future for both of us through her coming to work with me.

I listened attentively to understand who Charlotte was and what she was looking for. Reacting to nuances as much as to direct questions, I needed to judge whether she'd be a good fit for Stephenson Law as well as persuade her that we were amazing! From Charlotte's point of view, we were a new company that might fail. How would that look on her CV? She needed to be reassured that working for us wasn't a risk, and that we had great clients and interesting work.

When I first approached Charlotte with a connection request on LinkedIn, I could see that she was a great lawyer, and my opinion of her only grew during that meeting. Sounding as disillusioned with her career trajectory as I had been, we had similar values and it was evident she would be a wonderful addition to the business. I felt a sense of massive relief when she was persuaded that my vision was achievable and she was keen to be a part of it. Until then, while Corrine had helped out at the very beginning, there hadn't been another solicitor who had bought into the essence of what I was trying to achieve. I now felt more confident about the future.

Having been efficient in my communication of the logic and benefits of coming to work with Stephenson Law, I had effectively sold my vision to Charlotte. Although we would now work together as a team, I'd effectively persuaded her in exactly the same manner as if she'd been a client or any other stakeholder.

In any case, I was delighted to finally have someone working alongside me. It would no longer be the case that every piece of business had to pass through me. Due to the ever-growing volume of work, I had become a bottleneck, and Charlotte would alleviate some of that pressure. At the same time, I know that she, too, was happy to take an alternative pathway in her career at that time. It was a positive move for all concerned.

Coincidentally, after struggling for so long to find Charlotte, another qualified solicitor joined us shortly afterwards and by March 2019, Stephenson Law boasted a team of four lawyers. Like London buses, I waited an age for the first one…

Taking on new lawyers was imperative for allowing me to find the time and energy to develop the business and move forward. My objective had never been to own a small firm that no one would ever hear about or notice. I wanted to build a business that held its own. One that people would talk about because it was successful and different – the flamingo among the flock of pigeons.

I continued to work long hours, although with more staff and a growing client list. Flexibility for us all became more easily realised, and I made sure I was available to my children, too. Instead of having to cover everything in the office, I gradually delegated more and more of the legal work to concentrate on sales.

There had initially been a bit of uncertainty around my credibility when I first founded the firm; I was still considered quite junior at six years qualified. Being a woman as well, I'm sure I was dismissed out of hand by some potential early clients, although that soon changed as our reputation grew. Stephenson Law was good at what it did, and as our turnover increased, so did my confidence in our business model. As well as being super ambitious for the business to grow and succeed, I remained committed to challenging the way legal services were delivered.

Our clients could see – by the way we dressed and presented ourselves – that we looked different to most lawyers, too.

On one occasion, in early 2019, I was getting ready for a client meeting that I already knew was a big deal. It was a large company that needed support while a member of their legal team was on maternity leave, and I wanted to make a good impression. That morning, as I reached into my wardrobe for a conventionally smart outfit, I stopped myself. Instead, I opted for something more casual, something I would never have worn in my previous law firm days. After making my presentation, which seemed well received, the Head of Finance approached me. 'It's so refreshing to meet a lawyer that dresses like me,' she said. 'Someone who looks like they'll fit in with my team.'

Not only did we win the contract, but it was also a fabulous boost to my confidence. I'm sure there have been others who weren't so keen on my appearance, although I've been asked to recommend tattoo artists more times than I can remember. Being a predominantly youthful team, we often reflected the looks of the staff in the tech scaleups of our target market. These were positive attributes that helped demonstrate how we were a great fit for them to work with. We saw the world around us in a similar way and grasped that we were all innovators in our different ways. We were providing these young founders with legal expertise that was jargon-free and easy to understand. It was a pleasure to sell Stephenson Law to people I understood and who understood me. But despite it being enjoyable, I only did so when it was appropriate.

To me, it's obvious that trying to sell services to someone who doesn't need them is not a recipe for success. On the contrary, if you are honest and refuse to sell an inappropriate service, it will help build up trust. If ever that client needs your advice at some future date, you can be sure they'll come back to you. And if they never need your services, you can be sure they will speak highly of your integrity to others.

On occasion, I've been aware that a potential client is interested in working with me, but the timing isn't right. Once, I was approached to register a trademark, and I could see the company wasn't yet ready to commit to exactly what they wanted. Although determined the logo would include a lion, they weren't sure if it was going to be upright and suggest proprietorial ambition, or laying down to infer proprietorial confidence. 'Let's leave it for the moment,' I said. 'Wait until you've nailed down precisely what you want the message to be.' 'Why can't we get the ball rolling now?' They seemed aghast that I was effectively turning work away. But I wasn't. I simply knew they weren't quite ready and kept in touch enough so they didn't forget to come back to me, but not so frequently as to become a nuisance. Finally, they chose an elephant.

There have also been occasions when I know we're not the right fit for a client, and one of us will decide not to take things further. Unlike so many firms I've previously worked for, we don't promote ourselves as offering everything to everyone. Instead, we concentrate on what we're good at and reach out to those companies we think will fit with our thinking.

We've always been very sales and marketing-led. To me, this is how a business grows and sustains itself. It's always been about our brand, our content, and everything we stand for. From when I first took my vision and spent months creating a business plan, I knew it had to be coherent. It had to make sense for it to be presented, promoted and sold to the SRA as a desirable product. And I think that's the difference between a law firm run by lawyers and a law firm being run as a business. I may be a lawyer, but primarily, I see Stephenson Law as a business that sells a great product. Maybe that makes me more of an entrepreneur than a lawyer... although, to me, it just makes good sense.

PART THREE – MY VISION

11. Rapid Expansion

After nine months on the NatWest accelerator programme, we moved into a co-working office in central Bristol and, having taken on our first marketing professional, became a team of six. Business continued to flow in, so before long, we outgrew that space and moved into a nearby office that could accommodate twice the number of people. Having been in business for a couple of years, we'd become more known locally, and it was rewarding when a new lawyer, Ed Boal, told us it was our vision for change that had most appealed to him. Like me, he was convinced that allowing lawyers to be themselves and bring their individuality into their work was advantageous to all. Being better established meant others were talking about our way of doing things, and as a result, it was getting easier to attract new staff as well as new clients.

I was rapidly gaining knowledge as I went along, and continuing to reach out to potential clients to share what we could achieve together and hopefully build a future relationship with them. Convinced the ongoing mental endurance had to be comparable to climbing Everest, I was on a vertiginous learning trajectory where I frequently stumbled before picking myself up again. I soon discovered how it made commercial sense to win a client, and then continue working with them rather than just do one piece of work and off they go (while I have to find more business elsewhere). After all, it's much harder to go in cold and make a first sale than maintain a connection and build on it. Also, from a human point of view, it's so much better to have interactions with a client where you get to know them and understand their operation and future business plans. It's far more enjoyable for everyone.

As we grew, I encouraged our lawyers to create good personal relationships with our clients because it's more rewarding for them to draft contracts and not have to move on all the time to draft another one elsewhere. As a result of such good rapport, we have seen several of our lawyers go to work in-house for clients. That was always going to be a risk – although not one that has harmed us. Instead, it enhanced our reputation as a true in-house legal partner rather than merely a legal service provider.

In early 2020, we expanded further, and I began to feel quietly confident that my dream of a better way to deliver legal services was becoming a reality. I started to believe Stephenson Law would make it into the 30% cohort of new companies still in business after three years, and that my flamingo would grow into a beautiful and successful beacon for the legal world to admire. With a wonderful team of 12 supporting me, I was delighted to find a great new office and received the details of its lease in mid-March. It looked perfect for our needs, and I was just about to sign it when the world as we knew it came to a halt.

COVID-19 had taken hold in the UK.

The announcement of the first lockdown completely floored me. Along with countless other business owners, I could only see a future of doom and gloom for Stephenson Law; that the deadly virus would be the end of everything my team and I had put together over the previous three years. With conflicting reports in the media, nobody had much idea of what would happen in the medium or long term. All we knew was that we had to stay indoors.

There were daily TV bulletins from the government, but they seemed little more aware than the rest of us about our prospects. Of course, we now know that despite our Prime Minister becoming hospitalised with COVID, neither he nor many of those around him took much notice of the rules the rest of us followed. Like Emperor Nero in ancient Rome, they carried on partying while the world around them effectively burned. In any case, rather than signing a lease for new premises, I let our current lease expire and moved everything into storage.

We haven't had an office since.

My fear about how to keep the firm going was largely due to how integral face-to-face meetings had been in winning and keeping accounts until that time. Our clients were generally based in Bristol or London, and I was still going out of the office to meet lots of people in person and attend networking events. While we did have a digital marketing platform that we hoped had a great future, it wasn't where our primary sales were sourced. At the same time, although we'd been super flexible from the beginning about where and when our staff worked, we did tend to spend a lot of time in the office and enjoyed doing so. It was a friendly and supportive base that served us well for sharing information, learning new skills, brainstorming problems or simply enjoying a coffee and chat. Everything went into reverse pretty much immediately when lockdown was introduced on the 23rd of March 2020. We'd hit more than £1m in sales at the end of our second year, and instead of being confident in seeing that figure continue to rise, I was terrified it would plummet and disappear.

It was a desperately difficult time on all fronts.

As parents who could work remotely, Pete and I had to juggle our own demanding workloads along with homeschooling and looking after our two young children. Very disappointed by the paucity of online work or support their school or nursery offered, we wrote a list of what seemed most urgent each day for each one of us and tackled the item at the top first. When 'give the dog a walk' reached pole position, we would vie with one another as to who should do this 'vital chore' that guaranteed a short respite.

I couldn't be sure that Stephenson Law would survive, and without any official indication of when workplaces would be allowed to open up again, I saw only one option. With immediate effect, we'd make everything *permanently* digital. There was no plan to ever return to having a physical office. Staff working remotely was a necessity, and a platform for scheduling virtual meetings was already in place. Having used my personal profile on LinkedIn as a launchpad for approaching clients, I'd always seen it as a medium with great potential. No longer able to have in-person meetings with would-be clients, I started to look closely at what more the platform could offer.

As an individual, I began making frequent posts on my thoughts and perspectives about how my company was challenging the status quo of the legal industry and why that was necessary. I wasn't intentionally trying to create a personal brand for myself; it was more a case that I had things to say about my own views of legal stories and personal experiences that were inappropriate to be shared under the auspices of Stephenson Law. My 'Let's talk tattoos' post was in my name, as were comments and criticisms about how law firms are regulated because they were my personal observations, not those of my company. However, the response was overwhelming, and I soon realised I wasn't alone in my opinions. I was surprised to see how many people agreed with me because I'd always considered myself an outlier. Instead, I discovered my desire for change was shared, and by continuing to post regularly, in 12 months I'd built up a community of 20,000 like-minded people all over the world.

At the same time, the marketing team at Stephenson Law was growing successfully, too, especially after Jess – a social media guru – joined us. It soon became evident that the more visible I became, the more visible my business became. And more engagement brought in more business. I began to post regularly on TikTok and Instagram, too, until it became so time-consuming I decided to concentrate on LinkedIn and create a personal website instead.

This was when my own brand of Alice Stephenson came into being. By having a personal platform, I could write a blog, share articles, create videos, podcasts, and so much more. Given the restrictions of lockdown, it made sense that online communities strengthened both on personal and business levels. That was certainly my experience where the interaction between my own platform and that of Stephenson Law created ever-increasing interest from a broad spectrum of people and organisations across the country and beyond. Stephenson Law was gaining a lot of business directly through social media channels, and our need for good lawyers continued to grow.

Until COVID, in the same way I only seriously targeted regional businesses as future clients, people with whom I could meet for a coffee to take things further, I used the same localised tactic for recruiting talent. Despite encouraging staff to work from wherever was most convenient, it didn't seriously cross my mind to search nationally rather than around Bristol. At that time, the concept of hiring people from elsewhere was alien to small companies like mine. I was aware of one tech client who successfully recruited remotely, but I'd reasoned that was due to the nature of a technology business. It was almost as if I had a mental block because, while I was happy for people to work from home if that suited them, I still clung to the notion of being able to have face-to-face contact when needed. I'm only talking about a handful of years ago, and yet – in early 2020 – it was only giant corporations like BT and British Gas that routinely had people based in different locations. It was only when you rang these companies and realised you were speaking to someone in South Africa or India that you recognised these people were working remotely. The arrival of COVID rebooted my way of thinking!

As we settled into the model of no longer having a permanent office, I could see the positives of what COVID had forced upon us. It had effectively transformed the business for the better, and we were becoming stronger. Once we took everything digital, not only had it opened up a nationwide business market, it also meant we could employ lawyers from Liverpool, London, or Land's End. It didn't take long before it was evident my fears around how COVID and lockdown would harm the business were unfounded.

I began to understand how embracing change is perhaps the most important aspect of building a thriving law practice in today's world. The legal industry is renowned for its antiquated tech, conservative ideals, and agonisingly slow processes. As a start-up business, we needed to challenge those norms and offer a better, alternative solution if we wanted to flourish going forward. For Stephenson Law to succeed in its chosen market of pioneering technology, we needed to be like our clients: innovative and inventive in finding new ways to support them as they develop further.

With the company continuing to grow, I saw how adopting an innovative mindset extended beyond the day-to-day running of the business. This allowed me to think in a more agile manner, to view our service provision from the client's perspective. How could we tailor our legal services to better suit *their* needs? What were *their* priorities with regard to legal requirements? I began to consider services such as contract reviews where we could offer a fixed price or range of fixed prices. This was also when I first mulled over the possibility of turning our retainer service into a subscription that was more akin to the service our tech clients were offering. It was as if I needed to grow with the business, and learn to evolve and move forward constantly.

At the same time, innovation requires creativity and a willingness to take risks. This necessity is a key side-step from everything we've been taught as risk-averse lawyers, but the reality is that entrepreneurial growth relies on a willingness to explore unknown new territory. On some occasions, it will be in the direction of fertile land with bountiful returns. On others, despite undertaking full due diligence in advance, it will be arid and offer a negative yield.

During the first 12 months of COVID, we simultaneously focussed on growth and experimentation. We tried expanding in various directions both in terms of the type of client we worked with, and the areas of law we operated in. It seems strange now that we ever practised litigation or that – on one occasion – we represented a racehorse trainer in a claim for losses arising from contamination of horse feed from a supplier! Sometimes, though, it was very challenging, and I worried that we could be caught in the trap of growing for growth's sake. Things happened so quickly that it was important for me to be able to step back and think. I needed the time to ask myself questions. What is this going to achieve? Is it going to work? Sometimes, I found enough time to ask the questions without allowing the appropriate time to formulate the answers or listen to them.

After creating a small disputes team, I soon came to the conclusion that just because something is a brilliant idea doesn't necessarily mean it will work. There were times when I was guilty of having all these really good ideas that could have been very successful if I'd had the resources to make them work. Having appropriately experienced lawyers was always crucial, but the firm's infrastructure needed to be constantly updated to match demand, and this didn't always happen. Our operations team was continually developing better ways to ensure we communicated reliably and instantly with one another, and provided a seamless service to our clients.

I still have many ideas running around in my head that I'm convinced will be viable when the time is right and we have the right systems in place. From early on, I've wanted Stephenson Law to be a beacon in the world of LegalTech. But that is still a dream, and as well as planning for the future,

I've had to learn to be more disciplined and patient – along with being more open with staff – about where we are today, as well as my fears and concerns.

Nevertheless, as we grew, we recognised that we were most successful in both achieving our own goals and those of our clients within the tech industry. And, in particular, scaleups – rapidly growing companies that continually evolve as they expand to satisfy increased demand. This mirrored our own experience and may partly have explained why it worked so well. We couldn't have taken ideas forward, such as a legal subscription service, if we hadn't made an initial attempt that was tailored to meet demand. Unlike us, though, scaleups rely heavily on outside investment, usually in the form of venture capital. Many faced a massive challenge from COVID and the residual downturn in global growth. Anxious international markets began to push up interest rates and investors became more cautious. As clients' costs rose and their runways fast approached with no guarantee of further funding, we felt the knock-on effect, although I assured staff that a solid advantage of running a law firm like ours is that whatever happens to a company, as long as it stays solvent, it will continue to need legal support in one form or another. This may be to help prepare the business to be sold to another company or simply to slim its operation in the short- or long-term and lay off staff.

It is widely recognised that airlines laid off thousands of people when lockdown cancelled international travel, and the knock-on effect this had on countless other sectors was equally catastrophic. English language schools, valuable invisible exporters, relied 100% on foreign visitors being able to come and study in the UK. Some of these education providers had been successful businesses for decades when COVID restrictions removed their source of income overnight. They needed guidance in employment law when they had to fold, prior to the introduction of the government's furlough scheme. Helping these businesses close their doors made me ultra-aware that crises can appear from out of nowhere, although I saw no point in worrying my staff about what could happen in the future when the business was thriving during a time of uncertainty.

While always ambitious for Stephenson Law, I'd never wanted it to become one of those cloned full-service firms that wanted to provide every client with every piece of legal advice they could possibly need. I wanted to grow while remaining relatively niche, with a good network of reliable referral companies for legal specialisms we didn't offer. And by this time, although I was still the CEO, I'd made Ed a Director and Jess our Head of Marketing. They were there to help make sure we took sensible decisions. It was great to wind down with them at the end of each week for an online catch-up about what we'd achieved, and where we were going. The meetings were invaluable in helping me acknowledge and appreciate the perspective of others who had the same goal as me, and I felt very lucky to have them. By remaining specialist, we'd created a reputable brand through a great marketing strategy that, in turn, attracted great lawyers. We were working together as a law firm that valued people as the priority within the business and beyond.

I'm not just referring to legal expertise here, but attitude, work ethic, creativity, professional insight… the impact of people and how they're valued is so far-reaching it's hard to quantify. It's not easy to build a team that shares a vision as well as drives a business forward, and when that happens, it needs to be nurtured. Of course, peoples' lives move forward and no team will remain unchanged, but as the old adage goes, look after your people, and they'll look after your business. Our people and their wellbeing was my first priority, as it was for Ed and Jess.

In an industry where lawyers are traditionally given a target of billable hours over which they have no control, and the prospect of an annual bonus if it's reached, we had to find an acceptable alternative. I still needed to motivate my lawyers but didn't know how. What I didn't want was for them to have the Sword of Damocles hanging over their heads each month as I'd suffered as a junior lawyer. At the same time, I wanted to solve the conundrum of how to give clients clarity over fees at the beginning of a project. This was important to me, and even while we were toying with the concept of a subscription service, and offered a couple of fixed-price products, we were predominantly still charging an hourly rate. We aimed to give a pretty close idea of the final costs at the outset but, of course, this was effectively based on how many hours we anticipated a job would take. And yet, the whole point of Stephenson Law was to do things differently.

'Why not offer a different type of annual bonus?' Pete suggested one evening when, once again, I was muttering about how to motivate staff. As always, he was my muse and never-ending sounding board. 'It could be offered to everyone based on turnover and profitability rather than hours worked – whatever their role or salary.'

'If we want to carry on growing, we've got to reinvest heavily in the tech to structure it properly,' I replied. 'I'm pretty sure that whatever's left, it won't be enough money.' The last thing I wanted was to be in a position where I graciously offered an insultingly low sum of money to some brilliant people in thanks for their efforts.

We were in the dilemma of needing to plough profits back into the company to maintain our growth trajectory while also investing in our people to ensure they felt properly valued. Trying to motivate a wide range of human beings in different roles was one aspect of remote working I found very challenging.

Our eventual decision was the introduction of a share option scheme. Initially, this was just for directors, although it was later rolled out to everyone. I have always been open about my plan to grow the business until the right kind of exit arises. Stephenson Law was definitely my baby and is still the fledgling business I created and continue to cherish to the best of my ability – as I do for each of my offspring. Nevertheless, I've always trusted that the time will come when each of them will feel confident to strike out alone. The fledgeling flamingo will have grown and found strength in its beautiful broad wings to take flight on its own trajectory. It's still a long way off, and I don't know what route it will take – whether outside investment or an outright sale. Whatever the case, those people who choose to stay with Stephenson Law in helping it flourish will be well-rewarded for doing so. In the meantime, I'm still doing all I can on a daily basis to ensure its long-term success with a balanced and ethical rate of growth. This is my priority.

Previous parts of this book are a testament to the early years when I juggled legal work and the running of the firm. I was stressed to the point that my laptop was effectively attached to my right hand from dawn until dusk before being tucked under my pillow for a few fitful hours; it was unsustainable. While I successfully juggled both, I always ran the risk of failing to do justice to either role. When I was able to delegate the legal work through a number of key hires, including Ed, and the marketing to Jess later on, I began to focus solely on building the business.

This was pivotal in being able to look at the broader picture, to function and perform to the best of my ability in managing the company. That's not to say that I stopped being involved in client acquisition or relationship building; it was simply achieved in a different manner. I became more heavily involved in the strategy and growth of the business model that was in total opposition to that of a traditional partnership. We became more creative in how the business was managed and how it brought in work. Rather than wining and dining would-be clients, we leveraged my personal brand to grow the firm. I took the lead in bringing about change and publicising it. Whether through interviews and video forums with media outlets such as The Female Lead, Legally Speaking, The Business Leader or writing for Forbes magazine, I promoted our agenda and explained our approach and the value we offered our clients.

This allowed us to stand apart from the crowd. It has also permitted the heads of our legal departments to take true ownership of their spaces. I would never have become a specialist in financial regulation law, but we had a talented Head of Finreg who was; therefore, they were given the opportunity to truly own that space for the firm. As I talk about later, this degree of autonomy has been so successful for our Intellectual Property department that it's become an independent organisation rather than remaining integral to Stephenson Law. As the founder and CEO of the firm, I focus on my speciality: growing a challenger business within the legal space.

In the same way as my creative instinct was advantageous in my role as a lawyer, it was an equally important part of being the leader of a modern law firm. We're in the age where lawyers and clients are seeking more, while LegalTech and new modes of working begin to take hold. Without a sense of creativity and a willingness to innovate, it's incredibly difficult for a law firm to mark its territory in a notoriously competitive field. My endeavour has been to build a brand that's more interesting and engaging for clients, as well as an opportunity for motivated staff to give their best. The firm has been designed to empower individuals to work to their strengths, and the results saw us grow into a multi-million-pound firm in just four years.

12. Breaking Down Barriers

As well as allowing individuals the freedom to work to their strengths, one of my main objectives with Stephenson Law was to allow people the freedom to be themselves. To me, this has to be a no-brainer, and of mutual benefit to the employee and the business. I strongly believe that when a person – from whatever background, gender, culture or religion they come from – feels free to express who they are in the workplace, and are valued as themselves, they will be more ready to give their best in return. This mindset didn't exist in any traditional law firm I came across.

Being a woman and mother (and therefore someone who wanted a family life alongside a professional one) had been an unavoidable obstacle to my legal career. I could only imagine how I would have been treated should I have been a black woman, a practising Muslim, gay, transgender or 'other' in any obvious way. Or how much more difficult it would have been even to enter the profession with such a disadvantage. And yet, what do any of these things have to do with being a good lawyer?

My tattoos were another issue for employers that should never have had any bearing on their assessment of my ability as a qualified solicitor. 'We may have joined an ancient profession,' a junior partner once remarked on noticing a small tattoo through the cuff of my blouse, 'but aren't *tramp stamps* more indicative of the oldest profession?' He thought he was being funny, while it just confirmed my opinion of him being a prick.

Years later, I remember my first client call with Stephenson Law, where my tattoos were clearly visible, and while nervous about the reaction, I knew it was something I had to do. 'How cool to be working with a rockstar lawyer!' was the initial response, followed by, 'Love the tattoos! It's always been on my bucket list to get one'. Given that experience, I always encouraged staff to be open and display their body art because it's part of who they are.

On one occasion before COVID, when all job interviews were still face-to-face, I was seated opposite a young woman who had come for a trainee role. My body art was clearly visible, and as our discussion progressed, she confided that she'd removed a nose stud before our meeting in case such adornment would be perceived in a negative way.

'You did what?' I asked, throwing my hands into the air. I stood up and pointed to the doorway. 'The bathrooms are through there on the left'.

I knew how quickly nose piercings close up and directed her to where she could wash her hands before replacing it straight away. On her return, the little jewel on the side of her nose only enhanced the broad smile beneath. She appeared more confident as we continued the interview and I thought it sad how she had felt it necessary to remove something that made her feel better about herself.

In instances like this, it was easy for me to ensure anyone employed by Stephenson Law could be themselves at work, wear what they want, and display piercings or tattoos. However, I knew that whatever our ethos and internal practices were – or their appreciation by staff – such freedoms were barely being spread or even acknowledged in the wider legal world, where the concept of a 'human lawyer', namely a rallying cry against decades of stiff tradition, driven by people who want a more sustainable, more fulfilling, and more human way of existing in the profession, remains alien.

In a 2022 UK YouGov poll,[26] just 17% of British workers claimed to love their job, with 84% of working professionals feeling they have to hide parts of themselves. In another

---

[26] https://www.bcllegal.com/knowledge-base/from-the-team/much-british-workers-like-jobs-pay

study,[27] three in five employees felt pressure to conceal parts of their identity because they:

- don't want to make people uncomfortable (49%)
- fear being stereotyped (43%)
- don't want it to affect their career advancement (41%)
- fear discrimination (41%)
- don't want to damage connections with coworkers

This pressure to conform and conceal is heightened in women and minority groups, with an American study revealing that 83% of LGBTQ+ employees engage in 'covering behaviours' in work, followed by 79% of African Americans, 63% of Latinos, and 60% of women.[28]

In many respects, this pressure to conform is a global phenomenon, establishing a norm where work sees you leave a bit of you at home. So what's the impact of this?

Overwhelmingly, it's not good news. Countless studies reveal that conforming workplaces result in more flawed decision-making, less risk-taking, and less innovative ideas overall. In stark contrast, work environments that promote diversity in all its forms enjoy more creative decision-making and better revenue overall. In fact:[29]

- companies with gender diversity earn 41% more revenue
- ethnically diverse companies are 35% more likely to perform better

---

[27] https://www.jobsage.com/blog/authenticity-in-the-workplace-survey/

[28] https://docket.acc.com/does-your-workplace-encourage-conformity-or-authenticity

[29] https://www.fundera.com/resources/diversity-in-the-workplace-statistics#:~:text=85%25 of CEOs with diverse, likely to capture new markets

- diverse teams are 70% more likely to capture new markets

Perhaps one of the most stunning reveals is that when people are actively empowered to be their authentic selves at work, their performance can be beneficially impacted by up to 85%.

Being only too aware of these benefits, I always made sure to highlight our inclusive agenda when talking on social media and being interviewed for magazines or podcasts and incorporated it in blogs, webinars and online posts. At the same time, I was constantly looking for other opportunities to promote our beliefs and desire for change. So, when during COVID, a member of the team suggested I explore the possibility of entering the business for a nationally recognised legal award, I followed her advice.

It was a great idea, and once I started to search different legal and business awards, there were lots of possibilities. I was sure that one would offer the perfect opportunity for me to put Stephenson Law out there, and be judged on what it had already achieved as well as its aspirations. Unlike lots of other young businesses, we weren't just grinding through the pandemic but rapidly growing. Proud of what we were doing and wanting public exposure, I decided to aim high.

Just three years after founding the business, I made an entry into the industry's most prestigious annual competition, the British Legal Awards. The judges were among the most successful and influential lawyers in the UK, and I reasoned that whatever the outcome of our bid, they would know who we were. The application was in the Boutique Law Firm category, where I told the story of why and how my dream to run a different kind of law firm came true. I kept to the word count and went through it a dozen times to make sure every single word counted! And after making the submission, I did my best to forget all about it. As always, there was plenty to keep me busy.

Even so, when I saw we'd reached the shortlist, I got rather excited and couldn't sit down for more than a few seconds at a time. Somehow, it made all the hard work and angst of the previous years worthwhile. Our name was up there with the biggest in the industry, and I'd been able to tell it how I saw it for all the legal world to see.

The awards ceremony was in November 2020. As a lockdown event during COVID, it had to be a 'virtual' event that we all watched on tenterhooks from our various locations. Then, when it was announced that we'd won the 'Boutique Law Firm Award 2020', I started to jump up and down. The dog on my lap almost went flying, and must have wondered what I was doing to her as she got hugged tighter and tighter. I almost cried with happiness.

Hearing Richard E Grant describe Stephenson Law as a 'brilliant example for the profession', which shows that 'simple and effective charging models' can 'attract top clients and stellar growth' was beyond measure.

By this time, I'd built a reasonable following on social media platforms, and so had inevitably begun to attract a scattering of trolls to my posts. Discovering that even those who worked for top London firms could still be old-school misogynist lawyers with no more interpersonal intelligence than pond life, I'd grown a thick skin to accommodate their bullying insults. Nevertheless, it was a tremendous tonic on both a personal and professional level to have this validation from the very pinnacle of the legal industry. We'd been judged and come out on top with our message widely broadcast.

Around the same time as winning the Boutique Law Firm Award, I heard about the national Women in Innovation Award.

Innovate UK is the UK's national innovation agency, where the government supports business-led innovation with financial aid and expert advice. It covers all sectors and regions to help industries grow through the development and commercialisation of new products, processes and services. The Women in Innovation programme began in 2016 when it was noticed that only 1 in 7 applications for funding came from women. This was despite the fact that success rates between male and female entrepreneurs are largely equal. The Treasury then commissioned the NatWest Deputy CEO, Alison Rose, to lead an independent review of female entrepreneurship to help explain the disparity.[30]

Unsurprisingly, it found that a third of respondents felt being a woman had negatively impacted their career, along with the lack of visible role models, mentors or accessible networks. (The note on accessible networks reminded me of Lady Hale's comments about the legal profession and the dominant role male bastions such as London's Garrick Club continued to hold for aspiring lawyers.)

The more I read about the Women in Innovation Award, the more I realised it was something I related to. As a law firm founder and qualified solicitor, I'd come face to face with every barrier described, and the one thing I had always promoted was the legal industry's need to innovate.

I'd spent lots of time giving legal support to tech founders with their amazing development projects and seeing their innovative ideas come to life. And, as a law firm, we'd dipped our toe into a couple of small projects that had proved to be successful. However, despite having considered a more ground-breaking venture, such as using AI in an online legal

---

[30] Rose Review progress reports have since been published annually.

platform, we'd never had the financial security to dive in and take the risk. Now, though, the criteria for the Women in Innovation award seemed to offer the perfect opportunity for us to plunge in headfirst. At first glance, it seemed to have been tailor-made for someone like me!

On closer examination of the conditions for gaining the £50,000 award, and the background of some of the previous winners, I knew I had my work cut out. It was evident I'd be up against some incredible women with remarkable ideas. Having never previously applied for any sort of business grant, I soon realised there was an art to it that I needed to study and familiarise myself with. There was much more to it than the short story I'd put together for the British Legal Awards.

The application covered several aspects that, while detailed and to a degree tedious, made me consider exactly what I was asking for and why. Given that innovation was one of the tenets of my business, putting my arguments together concentrated my mind on what was both bold and achievable. Despite believing that Innovate UK and its women's award had been specifically designed for people like me, my biggest problem was avoiding overambition and what could reasonably be accomplished. I needed to follow a fine line to promote a pioneering scheme with confidence that was also feasible and realistic.

Many of the questions were about me personally – my vision and how I could be a leader in innovation. There was a strong focus on why I believed I could be a suitable role model; why I was special and worthy of the accolade. It certainly wasn't a time for modesty, and I was quite willing to do what it took to succeed. To me, this was another opportunity to challenge the status quo that held so much power in the legal industry and show a wider audience that we could offer an alternative.

I explained my desire to build a legal platform for start-ups and scale-ups that could provide quality and cost-effective legal resources. Describing our experience of working with companies that had failed to get appropriate advice in the early stages of starting a business – only to be presented with more expensive and time-consuming problems further down the line – I outlined the need for a new approach.

Entrepreneurs have a number of legal questions they don't know the answer to. Young firms need to make informed decisions to mitigate risk and better their chances of survival. However, for a number of reasons (including a strong fear of unknown potential costs), founders are reluctant to approach a law firm. Instead, they typically resort to using Google or asking their peers. As a result, they are usually presented with a wealth of conflicting and unreliable answers.

My desire was to fill the gap between using anecdotal informers such as search engines or 'crowdsourcing' people the business owners knew, and what was perceived as the prohibitive costs of dependable legal advice from a traditionally-regulated law firm. To me, there was a very real need to make micro-advice affordable and accessible to entrepreneurs in order for them to maximise their chances of success. I was convinced of a strong business case for Stephenson Law to develop a tech-based, cost-effective and reliable solution. The project I had in mind for my initial submission focussed on an AI-powered interface to respond to straightforward legal questions with straightforward, no-nonsense answers. We'd already been working on our alternative methods of delivery for some time, and access to both financial help and expert advice to help us along the way would be invaluable.

As well as demonstrating that I was the right 'Innovative Woman', I also needed to show why my business was worthy of the award… how it would help us achieve our goals and what we could do to 'give back,' to inspire and support future inventive leaders.

There was a lot at stake that would be of great benefit to us, including a whole package of support from PR to mentoring and coaching to help develop our project. I knew that even if we succeeded in gaining one of the 20 grants on offer, our scheme would almost certainly need to be tailored along the way. And that would be fine. It would be altered according to the advice of top software engineers and AI experts.

The advantages on offer were pretty obvious to me. Nevertheless, I needed to demonstrate my appreciation of them and how I was committed to playing an active role in making the most of the whole process. Although a requirement, for someone like me, this was a priceless gift rather than an unreasonable demand. Why wouldn't I want to meet and get to know other award winners, past and present, and learn about their state-of-the-art projects and their dream careers?

It was altogether a wonderful experience for any businesswoman and one I wholeheartedly recommend. Whether the founder of a multi-million-pound enterprise or the head of a social enterprise, the aim was to celebrate female entrepreneurs from all walks of life. Providing them with a platform to shout about their achievements and enthuse future generations of ambitious girls and women interested in building new businesses.

After putting together the substantial written submission during the autumn of 2020, I waited to hear if my bid was good enough to take me to the next stage. A couple of months passed before I heard back. I'd made it through to the shortlist and needed to prepare a presentation for a panel interview.

Poor Pete. He must have watched and listened to my presentation a dozen times. Always my greatest supporter, as well as an amazingly astute critic, he made sure I gave detail rather than simply read slides, and spoke steadily with varied intonation. And all at an appropriate pace.

When the day came, and despite my countless run-throughs, it was still stressful. A truly squeaky bum time. I had to go in front of a panel of industry leaders and explain why my business idea was worthy of their time and taxpayers' money, but Zoom chose to fail me and I wasted a full five minutes of my allotted time battling with its screen share function, before answering endless questions about me and Stephenson Law. Then, in March 2021, after another long wait, I was officially named as a 'Woman in Innovation'. On receiving this second affirmation for what we'd been working towards, all the effort became doubly worthwhile.

It was a great feeling to know that I was one of only two lawyers to win the award and thrilling to have the recognition and support to accelerate my vision. And it wasn't long before I realised how much I could benefit both personally and professionally by being surrounded by brave thinkers from other business areas. People I learned so much from.

Subsequently, I entered other competitions to raise the profile of Stephenson Law and further demonstrate what we were trying to achieve. Even if we weren't shortlisted, putting our name out there gave us public exposure and when we were shortlisted or won awards, the exposure was greater still. It also gave me the opportunity to meet influential people in business sectors that interested me, and from whom I could learn.

As Denzel Washington says about being held up as a black icon in a very white industry, there's more to me than being a woman in a male-dominated field. First and foremost, I'm an entrepreneur and am super proud of being shortlisted or among the finalists for a variety of Business Leader Awards, British Legal Awards, Go Tech Awards, Lawyer Awards, Legal Innovation Awards, Bristol Life Awards and Legal

Business Awards. Our most recent success was winning the 2023 Modern Law Awards in the category of Marketing and Communication Strategy of the Year. And that was won because Stephenson Law used different (and very effective) marketing and communication strategies. Not because I'm a woman.

Issues surrounding gender bring me back to the earlier part of this chapter, where I readily acknowledge other young lawyers will have faced more onerous barriers than me. Nevertheless, given that the legal industry is intrinsically associated with language and its correct usage, I can't ignore its pervasive and generic use of masculine nouns and pronouns. And this is despite English not being a grammatically-gendered language like French or Spanish.

I have been infuriated to receive letters that address me as 'Dear Sir' or the business as 'Dear Sirs'. Legislative documents uniformly use the male pronoun when referring to both genders, along with 'Chairman' in constitutional documents when 'Chair' would be more fitting.

Why is this important? The short answer is because it's unnecessary, inaccurate, reinforces historic gender stereotypes and is simply wrong!

A more detailed response refers to a 2012 World Economic Forum analysis that found countries with gender-inflected language are the most unbalanced in terms of gender equality. By contrast, languages – such as English – which allow gender to be marked with descriptions such as 'female doctor' and 'male teacher' hold the highest equality rates.[31] The point being that if we're not able to identify something as female, the assumption is that it's male and, therefore, reinforces our unconscious bias.

It may come as a surprise to learn that English legislation was gender-neutral until 1850, when Parliament passed an

---

[31] 'Invisible Women', Caroline Criado Perez

Act for 'shortening the Language used in Acts of Parliament'. It stated that masculine words in legislation should be 'deemed and taken to include women', allowing those writing legislation to use 'he' and 'him' to refer to people, whatever their gender.

The premise that 'male includes female' continued in legislative documents until 2007, when government policy finally changed to reincorporate gender-neutral language. It took until 2016, however, for the first top City law firm to ban the salutation 'Dear Sirs' from its letters and 2020 for another to remove 'gendered language' from its legal templates.[32]

Following the cumulative layers of anti-discrimination legislation that go back over a century, these bastions of the British legal system should be embarrassed by having maintained such outmoded practices for so long. They are among a myriad of subliminal messages that remind us all on a daily basis about who is in control. And working in the legal world, they are reminders of who does and doesn't fit the criteria of becoming a successful lawyer.

Even when City firms recruit women, people of colour, and those from diverse backgrounds, the vast majority of partners are still privately educated white men. As previously discussed, they feel safer offering the most interesting deals to other privately educated white men who, having experienced working on one big juicy deal, will be picked preferentially for the next one. And so much of the networking is done out of the office. Even when the prestigious Garrick Club is ignored, there are opportunities like invitations to golf tournaments and rugby matches. However good she is, the outstanding Muslim woman on the

---

[32] www.thelawyer.com

team doesn't get invited to Manchester United to meet the club's general counsel.[33]

Traditional legal partnerships are slowly coming to realise the need to modernise. However, given their long-established male-dominated hierarchy, which continues to serve them well, any measurable transformation is painfully slow. Companies like Stephenson Law, in contrast, not only lack the outdated history and hierarchy but were established to offer an alternative to meet today's demands and can react more quickly.

Our world is increasingly multi-cultural, multi-faith, multi-gendered and one in which I feel very comfortable. Technology has massively amplified the pace of change in recent years, and at Stephenson Law, we have tried to embrace this time of flux with our eyes open to future possibilities. Integral to all of this is our diverse team of lawyers, marketers and support staff. They hail from all corners of the UK and are valued for the variety of experiences and backgrounds they bring to the business. It couldn't exist without them.

---

[33] The Times Newspaper, January 1st 2023

13. A Different Delivery

From the moment I joined Reese & Able and first learned about how lawyers are paid and clients are invoiced, I felt certain there had to be a better option than the traditional billable hour system.

This straightforward method of pricing lies at the heart of most law firms, and the concept is simple: clients are charged by reference to the amount of time it has taken to provide the service required. An hourly rate, which reflects the level of expertise a lawyer possesses and their firm's position – vis-à-vis its competitors – is applied. Lawyers have to record the time they have spent on a specific job, often in six-minute units, to ensure it can be converted into cash. Clients are invoiced after the work has been completed or (on larger projects) in tranches in arrears as the assignment progresses. Neither party really knows at the outset what the final bill will be.

I've been in the legal industry for over 15 years, and throughout that time, the billable hour and most people's hatred of it has remained a constant. Clients and lawyers both recognise the fundamental flaws it presents, yet a seemingly insurmountable challenge prevents its demise. Nobody has worked out what to replace it with to the satisfaction of all stakeholders.

So, what makes it so unpopular? Having already alluded to some of its shortcomings in earlier chapters, let's now examine it in more detail. Firstly, let's look at it from a lawyer's perspective.

With the exception of a firm's senior partners, lawyers are typically measured by the number of billable hours they submit to be counted in a day, week, month and year. A utilisation rate is generated, providing visibility of how a lawyer is performing in comparison to their target and their peers, and this metric often directly impacts the progression opportunities made available to them. It makes sense if one individual is generating greater revenue for the firm than their colleagues, that they will be encouraged to continue in the same manner.

At first sight, this may appear to be a reasonable approach until consideration is given to how little control junior lawyers have over their workload. They are generally passed work from their senior colleagues, and the better their face 'fits', the more work they are likely to be given. The opportunities they encounter for progression are, therefore, directly linked to someone else's ability to generate work and the extent to which they fit the mould. As stated before, there is overwhelming evidence that white, privately educated males gain a distinct advantage, and while the system's proponents argue it is meritocratic, that is patently not the case.

The pressure to meet billable hour targets also acts as a deterrent to sharing work with colleagues, with individuals choosing to hold on to work to give them the best possible chance of meeting their target. This results in an unequal distribution of work in a dysfunctional team, where the best interests of a client are deprioritised over a lawyer's need to record enough billable hours.

Working with a client on an hourly rate basis is challenging. When a client is paying for every minute, they understandably want to see some justification for every minute, but clients often fail to appreciate how long it can take to do something that might, on the face of it, appear straightforward. For example, we were recently approached by a prospective client looking to pay £150 to find out if he could sell data he had accumulated through his own business activity. He thought it would be a simple yes/no, but the research and understanding that is needed to answer that question is far more time-consuming than he envisaged. In cases such as this, there can be lengthy conversations explaining how the time has been spent, and why it was a reasonable amount of time. Often, these conversations lead to time being written off and not charged for.

Amelia[34] works for an American law firm in London and has an annual target of 1,900 billable hours that she has to reach to earn her bonus, which represents around a third of her income. If she took her full holiday entitlement (less than if she worked for a UK firm) and didn't work on any weekends, it would mean she had to bill around 8 hours each day. However, there are obviously other work obligations and training necessities to keep up to date with current legislation that cannot be billed to a client.

'Realistically... I would normally try to work from 7am to 6pm, Monday to Friday, but it's not unusual for people to work 90-100 hours in a week,' she said. 'I pay... other people to look after my children for 11 hours a day...The expectation is that if you're working, you're going to carry on working over and above whatever your other plans were.'

This is exactly the work environment that I found unreasonable and unacceptable at Barracuda, but is what lawyers tolerate to further their careers in 'prestigious' firms. Even Amelia, having made the conscious decision to move to the role from having originally trained as a barrister, admits, 'If we were all happy and healthy and well adjusted, we probably wouldn't hit 1,900 hours a year.'

It seems ridiculous to me that in a wealthy and civilised society, a business model is designed in such a way as this. One that effectively creates an unhappy, unhealthy and maladjusted workforce.

This leads us to billable hours from a client's perspective and how that can be problematic, too.

In most marketplaces, whether shopping for food in a supermarket, shares on the stock exchange, or a car from a

---

[34] The Times Newspaper, January 1st 2023

dealership, the product has a price that the buyer agrees to pay the seller. Where the product is a service rather than an object – such as obtaining insurance against theft from a broker or having root canal treatment from a dentist – the customer or patient still knows what the bill will be in advance and, if something changes, maybe because you move house or there are unforeseen complications with the root canal, the price will change. People like to know how much something is going to cost before committing to purchase it. They can budget for it and know how it will affect their financial situation. This is a reasonable expectation. And yet, as a general rule, it's one that the legal industry rarely offers its clients.

Instead, law firms typically charge according to the amount of time a particular lawyer has spent, or a group of lawyers have each individually spent – often at differing hourly rates – on providing legal expertise. Why? Because every lawyer is different, and even if two lawyers with equivalent experience and hourly rates executed the same process, it's highly unlikely they would both spend the same amount of time working on the same piece of work.

The difference in time is perfectly reasonable given that, whether or not they are considered automatons, lawyers are human beings. And human beings have foibles. Reflecting on a legal framework with reference to a client's situation frequently requires a lot of thought, and if the lawyer is tired, stressed or repeatedly interrupted, it will take longer than if they are well-rested and relaxed with no distractions.

Of course, these aren't variables over which the client has any control, and yet it is the client who will be the one picking up the bill and having to manage the uncertainty they create. Is this fair, consistent or reasonable? My answer is unequivocally 'No'.

I would go further to argue that, ultimately, the way in which the billable hour is used within firms rewards inefficiency. It offers no incentive for the lawyer or law firm to be efficient because the longer it takes to complete a piece of work, the more they can charge for it. In addition, it relies heavily on the integrity of individual lawyers. I know from experience how lawyers, when worried about meeting their monthly target, can be tempted to overstate the time spent on a job and hence avoid recrimination from their superiors. In short, it encourages both incompetence and dishonesty.

From a client's perspective, the lack of cost certainty created by the various factors impacting what they will finally be asked to pay makes instructing a lawyer a very unappealing proposition. Nevertheless, traditional law partnerships continue to centre their culture around the billable hour and see no problem with it. They fail to see how the world around them is evolving and that attitudes change accordingly. Whilst there will always be a time and a place for the billable hour, new pricing methods are needed for today's more discerning clients who aren't afraid of searching the internet to see if they can obtain the information they need without paying anything. While we'd like to think we're not competing against those with a law degree from Google, the reality is that for a lot of early-stage businesses, it's the first place they turn to. When a young company is building an online presence and wants to upload a music clip to add character to their new website, they search online to see what's available. While there are numerous free music libraries, it can appear just as straightforward to download a short extract from a source that doesn't have the legal right to do so. Music copyright is a minefield and can depend as much on the interpretation of a piece as its composition or length. For example, while Beethoven's Fifth is so old that the original composition is out of copyright, if a recent recording of a modern arrangement was downloaded for any commercial use, it would almost certainly infringe copyright.

I acknowledge it isn't easy for law firms to get their pricing strategy right whilst making their services affordable for young companies and making a profit. And trying to accurately scope the work required to accomplish certain tasks is as good as impossible. Nevertheless, there are some standardised tasks that can be accurately costed for clients to know beforehand.

After much soul-searching and investigation into how we can offer our clients a fairer system, and our lawyers a kinder system, I've reached the conclusion that the billable hour, in itself, is not fundamentally flawed. Instead, it's the application of it within law firms that creates the issues just described. By putting so much emphasis on billable hour targets when it comes to the performance appraisal, law firms fail to acknowledge and reward all the other ways their lawyers add value to their businesses. A toxic environment is created whereby the worth of a lawyer is almost solely attributed to how many billable hours they've done in the last six months, and it doesn't matter if they've mentored a junior lawyer through a challenging period, or identified a process improvement that dramatically increases profitability. Naming and shaming those failing to meet their targets is a technique commonly used to apply pressure, yet no understanding is sought for the reasons why this might be the case.

At Stephenson Law, the billable hour does form part of our pricing strategy, but we adopt a very different approach from most other law firms. For us, the billable hour is one of several metrics used to assess the business and individual lawyer's performance. It's a tool that can help us to identify issues within the business, such as not having enough work, or the work not being equally distributed, which we need to address. But at the very heart of it are three important tenets: trust, transparency and teamwork.

Trust. I trust my team until they give me a reason not to. I trust that if they have work to do, they'll do it, which means I don't need to use the billable hour as a stick to force them to do what I'm already paying them to do. Equally, our clients need to trust that we're acting in their best interests or we'll have to waste large amounts of time justifying every minute we've spent. Whilst the billable hour may encourage inefficiency and therefore plant the seed of distrust, it doesn't mean that inefficiency is inevitable. Innovation and continuous improvement feature in everything we do, and the drive to do things better overpowers any drive for inefficiency that the billable hour might present.

Transparency: it's not actually the billable hour that clients hate. It's surprise invoices and an inability to budget. This can be so easily resolved with communication, but the legal industry has long had a communication problem. We regularly speak to our clients about fees and promise not to send them any invoices they're not expecting.

Teamwork: I've fostered a culture where teamwork is encouraged and rewarded and overshadows any temptation to hoard work to meet billable hours targets. I reject the notion that lawyers should be promoted merely on their ability to generate and complete client work. When I make decisions about promotions and pay rises, an individual's ability to lead and work as part of a team is far more important than the number of billable hours they've worked.

Something at the forefront of the legal industry (and particularly popular with our scale-up tech clients) has been our subscription services. Our core product is our Flamingo subscription, which we've modelled on the SaaS (Software as a Service) subscriptions offered globally online. So, whether you're buying into Netflix, Microsoft Office or our Flamingo subscription, you know what you're getting, what you're paying, and how often.

We've put together monthly, quarterly and annual options where subscribers sign up for a set amount of legal work that is purchased in advance. The client can call upon any of our team across all specialisms and be assured of accurate expert advice on demand, whether it's on employment law one day, data protection the next, or intellectual property the day after. Our subscription clients are guaranteed same-day responses and clear timelines for work, with all pricing crystal clear. If the amount of work is more than what has been signed up for, they will be informed of any costs before they are incurred above their allotted subscription fee. It effectively provides clients with a cost-effective, bolt-on legal team to ensure they are equipped with practical, commercial advice that provides them with legal solutions rather than legal blockers.

Stephenson Law broke away from the legal industry's long love affair with ancient tech because I felt certain the time had come for it to move forward into the 21st century. We're not only in the digital age, but we're also watching the rise of LegalTech and AI, which is beginning to come into its own within the industry. In the same way as email changed the way we do business every day, AI will become an indispensable assistant to every successful lawyer. Those who choose to ignore its importance will get left behind, while those who use it will be freed up with more time for thinking about a client's needs, giving appropriate advice and delivering it efficiently.

What we have done and are trying to do better all the time is package up services and sell them as a product by embracing appropriate technological advances as they become available. Creating, promoting and providing a package of services as a product is a very different way of marketing and delivering legal services, and our journey certainly hasn't been plain sailing. But, given our subscriptions' popularity with clients, and seeing other firms follow in our footsteps, we know the principle is robust.

I'd always aimed at offering an alternative to the conventional procedures favoured by old-fashioned legal partnerships, but I've only discovered the advantages of being different through experience. Our singular style of branding, marketing and approach has been crucial through difficult times when I've been trying to carve out a space as a challenger law firm. And I've come to the conclusion that our decision – to be a tech-driven law firm – should be fundamental for anyone looking to start a thriving law practice today. I've discovered that by implementing tech innovations throughout the business, I've not only made my job easier but also that of our lawyers and our clients' lives too. Whether it's automating lengthy admin, dramatically improving the storage of data, or saving clients from infuriating paperwork – by leveraging technology – I've succeeded in ensuring our services are competitive both in quality, price and delivery.

Our decision to leave all staff working remotely after COVID was also a game-changer for us. Pete and I even emigrated when it dawned on us that we could! While living in Amsterdam had always been one of those longed-for dreams, we doubted it would ever happen until it became a possibility during the first lockdown in 2020.

Along with other young families, we were faced with homeschooling our two young sons when lockdown hit. We assumed the boys' school would provide a fair degree of teaching support for us to implement remotely, but we were wrong and very much left to our own devices on how to keep the children occupied and stimulated. Then, just as the government introduced measures to help businesses and individuals manage financially, our landlord informed us of a substantial rent increase.

Instead of simply accepting the situation, when the restrictions were lifted in the summer of 2020, we decided to move to the Netherlands. Although it took a little getting used to, we've never regretted the decision to offer ourselves and our children the opportunity of living elsewhere and in a city that exhibits many of the principles we hold dear.

Pete's life as a PhD candidate has continued in the same vein as if we'd remained in Bristol, and watching how easily our boys have fitted into a different culture has been a pleasure. As a student with a penchant for international travel, Lydia also welcomed the move. With regard to my role at Stephenson Law, whether I've spent the last few years in the UK or the Netherlands has been of no consequence. The Eurostar service from Amsterdam to London is more reliable than that of the GWR from Bristol, the cost is remarkably similar during busy periods, and I can cycle to the *Centraal* station in less than 15 minutes from our apartment.

When I read about firms insisting their staff return to the pre-COVID routine of commuting daily to an office, I'm amazed they don't offer at least some choice of working from home. Being based remotely suits so many people, particularly parents who can pick the children up, sort out dinner, and still be able to get all their work done easily because they no longer spend two hours a day travelling.

At the same time, I do recognise the advantages of working in an office where just having other people around and getting out of the home can be beneficial. If someone is struggling with health issues, either mental or physical, others are much more likely to notice and be supportive if they're in the same place. Training is easier to undertake face-to-face, and I know various team members in London, Bristol, and Newcastle choose to meet up either in a co-working space or elsewhere on a regular basis. We've also interviewed people for different roles who have turned down good positions because they didn't want to work remotely. Equally, others have approached us specifically because they know that's our model and it works for them.

It's a different approach that has allowed us to tap into a far wider recruitment market than if we were geographically static and, in keeping with my flamingo branding, makes us stand out from other law firms.

We're definitely leading the way in innovative practices that are being emulated by others who are finding them much more difficult to implement. This is because we developed our system of remote working and packaging up legal services across a variety of disciplines as we grew. It's in our DNA and integral to our USP. In the same way, our marketing approach developed into a totally different strategy to what was traditionally perceived as effective for legal companies.

I'm a big believer in the power of marketing to achieve great things, but it's not something all lawyers are comfortable with. They're so used to brochures, pamphlets and branded pens (although I do love a good quality branded pen!) that they overlook the opportunities now available to everyone in the modern online world. Historically, the responsibility for generating new leads and building relationships fell to senior partners – often on a golf course or over a lengthy lunch. Nowadays, though, with tools like LinkedIn, Instagram and Twitter, everyone can become involved in sharing the company's message and help bring in more business. In my experience, a lot of would-be customers are jaded by the corporate marketing of days gone by and are seeking something new, fresh, and innovative.

Yet, as lawyers, we're expected to be sombre and stern, prioritising professionalism at all costs. From suits to leather briefcases, there's a clear image in the public's mind when they think of a lawyer that's a million miles away from social media. And for many lawyers, the thought of descending into TikTok is career suicide. Many believe that building a creative brand online is detrimental to their credibility and will lose them business clients. They overlook the demographics of the various platforms and associated businesses, from the corner hairdresser to every Premier League football club post on Instagram and Facebook. And while I'm sure lawyers are as likely to use Airbnb, Uber or Deliveroo as anyone else, how do they think these mega-businesses first gathered interest if not through online branding?

For Stephenson Law, the benefits of social media have far outweighed any negative experiences. I've gone viral on TikTok, I've shared my most personal thoughts on Instagram, and I've sparked mass debate on LinkedIn. The result? Clients have come to Stephenson Law for our relatability, our willingness to speak hard truths and our human-first approach. And because they feel like they know and trust me, even if they've never met me.

I remind myself that there are few things worse in business than fading into obscurity, and have always worked hard to keep my trusty flamingo standing head and shoulders above the crowd. That doesn't mean we've always come out on top. Nor does it mean I've always made good decisions, even if they were made in good faith.

14. My Annus Horribilis

We entered a new financial year at the beginning of April 2022, and I was brimming with optimism. It was hard to believe how far we'd come in less than five years, and I couldn't help but feel a sense of achievement. With barely enough hours in the day to keep up with everything demanded of me, and almost having to diarise mealtimes with my kids and Pete, it was nevertheless pretty amazing.

With lawyers, operations and marketing staff based around the UK and me at the helm in Amsterdam, we seemed to be moving at a fair pace and on an even keel (although we couldn't be exactly certain of where we were heading). Our provision and supply methods were still evolving, but Stephenson Law was already a stand-alone example of how legal services could be delivered successfully in a different, more humane way.

Having nearly doubled our turnover in the previous two years, I was confident that we could further increase it from £3m to £4.5m in the coming year. Looking more closely at our legal team and various income streams, we already had the potential to deliver £4m, so with planned expansion in specific areas, it felt well within our grasp.

Cash flow had never been an issue previously, and I was confident that our strategy with supporting financial targets and projections was robust. It was time to invest in our infrastructure, as the current systems and processes were crumbling under the weight of the recent expansion. A key part of this was an exciting platform we were already building to onboard clients more efficiently, which now required additional technical support to bring online. We also needed to grow the marketing team to help us reach the extra £1.5m in sales. So, we made a recruitment plan and started hiring.

A year later, in April 2023, I couldn't believe how naïve and uninformed I'd been about so many aspects of the business. Even when it became obvious that we needed to retreat, regroup and re-evaluate, I blithely soldiered on. I was blind to battles being fought and lost that were way beyond my control or that of our clients.

The first near-fatal blow arrived in June 2022 when, as a regulated law firm, we had to renew our professional indemnity insurance. We began the process the same way we'd approached our previous renewals and sent all the required information to our broker so they could obtain quotes for us.

The only one we got back was from our existing insurer, and seeing the number of '0's after the '2' made my heart miss a beat. It was for £200,000. How on earth could this be right? The legal work we were carrying out was generally considered low risk and in the five years we'd been in business, we'd never made a claim. Or even considered making a claim. I rang our broker.

'You won't get a better quote,' he told me. 'There's been a ground shift in the market.'

'Ground shift?' I asked. 'We're working in exactly the same market as last year.'

'No, not your market. The global market,' he replied. 'It's because of the Ukraine war.'

Without indemnity insurance, we couldn't carry on trading, so I had no choice but to accept the quote, although we didn't have £200,000 languishing in a bank account. Along with many other law firms, we'd always worked with a finance company to advance our annual premium and we'd never encountered any problems. Rather than keep money in the bank, we preferred to reinvest as much as possible into the company with intentionally low profit margins as a result. Despite the frighteningly high quote, I had no reason to believe we wouldn't be able to cover our insurance costs as in previous years. I was wrong.

One sunny Monday morning, when the birds were merrily chirruping among the bright green leaves of the tree outside my window, and just five days before our insurance needed renewal, I heard back from the finance company.

'We very much regret that on this occasion we will be unable to advance the necessary funds…'

Momentarily panicked, I felt as if this was some sort of premonition until my fear turned to annoyance. Convinced there had been an oversight or misunderstanding, I rang them.

'It's got to be a mistake, and it needs to be sorted.' I tried to control my anger. 'We're legally obliged to have this insurance.'

Didn't they realise how important it was? Stephenson Law would have to cease trading if it wasn't in place by the end of the week.

'There is no mistake,' came the reply. 'Our underwriters are concerned your company is no longer profitable.'

'Not profitable?' With a lump in my throat, my fury switched back to fear. How could that have happened?

'Well, not profitable enough for us to advance such a large sum.'

My head was spinning as I put down the phone. It didn't make sense. Even if our profitability was down, surely we were very low risk?

I went into overdrive. Working with our Head of Finance, we rapidly prepared financial statements to approach all the finance providers I could find. And I vowed to myself that I would never allow an insurance company to have the power to shut down my business again.

After a series of sleepless nights, I woke up on the Friday morning filled with anxiety. None of the other finance companies we'd approached would lend to us. My only option was to persuade the one who at least knew us, even if they'd initially declined us.

I rang them again, and – after a few stressful hours – they finally agreed to make the loan. At more than double the previous year's rate of interest and with the proviso that one of my co-directors and I offered personal guarantees should the business fail. Far from ideal, it was nevertheless a solution that enabled us to keep going.

While hating the fact that such administrative agony could have stopped us from trading, I was still optimistic that Stephenson Law would continue its trajectory of year-on-year growth. After all, why wouldn't it?

Back in 2011, I had to move firm immediately upon qualifying as a lawyer when the international banking crisis drove Reese & Able to reduce its workforce. It demonstrated how decisions taken by our government, or others from across the globe, can have serious consequences for each and every one of us. Having paid a heavy personal cost as a direct result of others' misjudgements regarding sub-prime mortgages in North America, the idea of politics not being important, of interest, or affecting me was no longer the case.

The political decision to lock down the country during COVID had an immediate impact on us all, with lingering after-effects and costs that may last for decades. While its short-term significance on Stephenson Law and our remote working practice was positive, it also played havoc with international trade and helped precipitate a global recession. The angst I suffered in 2011 paled into insignificance with what was forced upon me through much of 2022 and 2023.

At the beginning of 2022, businesses in the UK and elsewhere continued to enjoy very low bank interest rates that had largely been in place since the 2008 financial crisis. Post-COVID, it was hoped that any inflation would be short-lived, interest rates would remain low and international business would soon be back to normal. However, while China was still struggling to get its mammoth production lines of plastic bags, PVC windows, computers and clothing back on track, Russia decided to invade Ukraine.

Russia is the world's largest exporter of oil and gas, while Ukraine is widely known as the 'breadbasket of Europe'. Unsurprisingly, the hostilities caused a hike in the global price of all fossil fuels and food that drove up inflation massively. Governments then increased interest rates in response. In December 2021, the Bank of England's base rate of interest was 0.25%, having been less than 1% since 2009. A year later, it was 3.5%.

The majority of our client base is made up of tech businesses and, in particular, tech scaleups that rely heavily on venture capital investment. Each time their investment costs increased in 2022, they had to reassess their business models. The worst-case scenario was that the business went to the wall, and in every other case, budgets got slashed – including legal budgets.

This was apparent when, in early July, we could see how much we'd fallen short of our financial targets for our first quarter (April, May and June). We'd recently hired a new Head of Finance, and when I turned to him for advice, he assured me this was little more than a rough period. While the figures were obviously disappointing, he was convinced that we'd see a marked improvement by the end of the second quarter. Taking this to the Board – instead of looking at the larger picture – we decided we could turn the figures around if we hired a Head of Sales. So that's what we did.

Just a few days later, I awoke to a series of panicked messages from Laura, my Head of Operations and longest-standing employee. The night before, she'd received an anonymous message informing her that our Head of Finance wasn't who we thought he was. I immediately spoke to her, and she'd done some digging in the meantime.

'I think he may still have been in prison when he applied for the job,' explained Laura, and how he'd been jailed for stealing £500k from his previous employer and been struck off as a Chartered Accountant. When she finished talking, we both remained silent, simply staring at one another through Zoom. We were probably thinking exactly the same thing.

Oh. My. God.

As soon as the working day began, I invited him to a meeting where he admitted everything. He explained that his registration as a Chartered Accountant had only been removed after going to prison, and so he'd been keen to find a new position before it had filtered through and any potential employer discovered the truth through due diligence! He was fully aware that a regulated law firm could never have a Head of Finance with a criminal background. The audacity and dishonesty were mind-blowing.

That was the first time I dismissed someone on the spot.

Overnight, we'd somehow morphed into a business experiencing serious challenges and a significant volume of day-to-day financial needs with minimal financial support. We also had to tell our regulatory authority, the SRA, what had happened so they could investigate how we'd managed to employ someone with a criminal record. Another first, and not something I would care to repeat.

This work-based drama coincided with the discovery that the au pair who'd been living with us for the previous five months to help look after our boys had been stealing cash from our bank account. There were lots of small transactions that Pete and I had assumed were made by each other that added up to a significant amount.

That was my second experience of dismissing someone on the spot.

With my faith in humanity hanging by a thread, we muddled through as best we could at home and appointed an external accountancy firm for Stephenson Law while we looked for a new Head of Finance. I wasn't surprised when we uncovered various issues with how our outgoing Head of Finance had been running things. Fortunately, there was no theft, although he wasn't as on top of things as he'd led me to believe. This may have been partly because he was working for another company as their Head of Finance at the same time, as we later discovered!

Throughout all of this mayhem, I was forever grateful to be supported by Pete at home and by my co-directors, Ed, Jess and recently appointed non-executive Iouri, at work.

I always felt that Ed was my legal alter ego and had been intrinsic to how Stephenson Law had developed from early on. We had a shared vision for our chosen industry, although sometimes locked horns with smiles on our faces about how to achieve the end goal. It was Ed who so generously agreed to co-guarantee our insurance loan. Jess was one of our earliest social media marketing specialists, and growing with the company, I couldn't imagine anyone else more in tune and capable as our Chief Commercial Officer. Iouri, our very own 'techie', was still relatively new to the Board but adding tremendous value and support. And whether we liked it or not, his unflinching message about how we needed to see, understand, and keep on top of the day-to-day business figures was starting to make sense.

As we approached the end of our second financial quarter, it became clear that the summer months had been quieter than expected, causing us to fall even further behind target. With talks of a recession on the front pages of newspapers, our turnover figures were no better than a year earlier. At the same time, our costs had grown significantly, and as a Board, we knew something had to be done. Alongside exploring the options available to take us out of the regulated space and avoid another crisis at our next insurance renewal, we adopted a two-pronged approach of cutting costs and driving sales.

Until then, we had never needed to consider redundancies. When we'd previously 'shrunk back', it was more a case of gradually pulling away from one direction that wasn't going well and turning our attention to another. However, this was different. We could see where we were making money and where we were losing it. Over the previous months, the global cryptocurrency market bubble had exploded. Bitcoin, which had been trading at over £50K towards the end of 2021, had dropped in value by nearly 75% in 8 months. We resolved to no longer offer expertise around cryptocurrency and blockchain laws or regulation.

In September 2022, we took the difficult decision to make our blockchain team redundant and effectively cut our staff by just over 10%. While it also reduced our turnover by around 15%, the accounts suggested that the measure would increase our profitability sufficiently to see us through the general downturn in business growth.

Emotions ran high as we redesigned the structure of the firm and decided which individuals we would have to let go. Putting personalities to one side and focussing purely on roles wasn't something that came naturally to me or my co-directors.

We'd never done anything like it before and hadn't anticipated how those five redundancy notices would shake every member of staff to the core. Because nobody, other than my co-directors, had any idea we were in trouble.

It had always been my mantra to shield staff from bad news whenever possible. Partly because I didn't want to burden them unnecessarily and partly because I didn't want to frighten anyone into handing their notice in. This had clearly been a poor management decision, given the panic created by the redundancies, which immediately precipitated an influx of resignations from people we didn't want to lose. I thought back to that beautiful June morning just a few months earlier when I had my momentary premonition of fear. Now, I seemed to have transitioned into being permanently mired in it.

With fingers crossed, we headed into the autumn with Ed and Jess doing their best to boost morale and build confidence in their respective teams. Iouri concentrated on creating a platform to show us precisely where we were in terms of our ongoing profit and revenue situation so that we could manage our finances much better. I turned my attention to avoiding a different crisis when our professional indemnity insurance came up for renewal in 2023.

I'd always been aware that the 2007 Legal Services Act meant that law firms no longer had to be owned and run by lawyers or regulated by the SRA. When I founded Stephenson Law in 2017, I took what I felt was the most likely pathway to long-term success and chose to be regulated. I thought it gave us more gravitas and that people would take us more seriously. Now, though, after much consideration of our role as a challenger firm and the market route we found to be the most rewarding, I began to look at the alternative. An alternative that didn't demand the prohibitive cost of indemnity insurance. None of our main activities necessitated regulation or were deemed high risk.

I reminded myself that being a regulated firm offers clients the peace of mind that comes with rigorous compliance practices and a formal complaints procedure. If grievances can't be resolved, clients can make their case and ask for the Legal Ombudsman to intervene, if necessary. However, when I searched into the detail, I found that clients were generally as happy with services provided by unregulated firms as those that were regulated. It also indicated that unregulated firms were more likely to be innovative in their method of delivery, transparent with costs, and cheaper! I came across a report from the Legal Services Board[35] back in

---

[35] Law Society Gazette, June 2016

2016 that said, overall, unregulated providers brought greater access, choice, and fairness in the supply of legal services.

This made my mind up, and when I shared my findings with the Board, we were all in agreement.

Ever since the nightmare with our outgoing Head of Finance, we'd been trying to find a suitable replacement. We needed someone who was willing to take the leap of faith necessary to join a company that wasn't in the best of shape. In addition, they needed to display excellent cash flow management skills – and convince me of their honesty! It was a big ask, and finally, towards the end of the year, it looked like we'd found that special person. We looked forward to Mairead starting in January.

At the Board meeting in early December, we agreed to try and have the third quarter's sales figures ready before Christmas, as nothing would happen between then and New Year's Eve. Iouri thought his new platform, Supo, would be ready in time for us to have up-to-date information and give us a head start on where we'd need to focus. It wasn't a joyous occasion, but we were all feeling a bit more confident about the future and raised a glass to welcoming our Mairead and a better 2023. I was very much looking forward to relaxing over Christmas and being able to enjoy a proper break with Pete and the children.

Getting dressed one morning, a few days later, I noticed my reflection in the mirror. Despite my smile on seeing the beautiful bright tattoos I so loved, the strain of the previous months seeped through. I appeared drained, with my shoulders sagging under the weight of every one of my 41 years. I straightened my back, took a deep breath and reminded myself of how lucky I was in so many ways. Staring into my own eyes, I was determined to get into the spirit of the season with my wonderful family and revel in Amsterdam's amazing festive traditions. So, I took another deep breath, smiled again and went in search of some breakfast.

The bombshell fell just as the boys broke up from school for the holiday. Iouri's platform was live, and he sent through the third quarter's figures. They were accompanied by a full explanation of the spreadsheets showing our daily cash flow situation vis à vis previous periods, plus a profit and loss report. It was evident that the September redundancies weren't going to be enough.

Our revenue streams remained at 2021 levels, and although our costs had gone down, they hadn't dropped sufficiently. For us to survive the increasing pressures from high inflation and interest rates, we needed to cut back again.

I hated having the news delivered just as I was hoping to have some fun with my boys. At the same time, I knew it was good to be able to mull the situation over properly during the Christmas and New Year break and consider what to do next.

My co-directors had also received the report prior to a pretty glum Board meeting I chaired at the beginning of January 2023. The only important item on the agenda was yet another rethink of our costs and sales strategies.

I had to rationalise further restructuring, which everyone knew was simply a euphemism for cutbacks. As I outlined my suggestion for more staff redundancies, I could see the colour drain from Ed's face. It worried me, but what was the alternative? Surely, he could see that we had no choice.

'This has to be the most difficult time since I founded Stephenson Law,' I said. 'The big problems early on were about how to cope with the amount of work coming in. Now, it's the opposite. It's overheads we can't afford.' I went on to argue that as lawyers generated our core revenue, they had to take priority over others. Jess's head jerked, and I could sense her growing unease.

'It's not just our own financial situation that's bleak,' I swallowed before continuing. 'Whether you read the FT, the Wall Street Journal or look at IMF predictions, global economic predictions for the coming year are crap. We can't just sit back and watch while everything we've worked for goes down the pan.'

Every word I uttered was the truth, and I'd hoped to see a flicker of amusement on others' faces at my intended pun. A sign they understood where I was coming from. That we were still all on the same side. But only Iouri, whose work had highlighted what we were discussing, responded with a painful smile.

The meeting dragged on as we scrutinised the minutiae of the figures and what they meant. We checked they aligned with the business accounts and bank balances. They were devastatingly accurate.

We agreed to convene again the following day after making personal assessments on which members of our wonderful staff would have to go.

After a number of tough meetings, we sent out a handful of redundancy notices to support staff. We also wrote to each member of staff outlining what had to be done and how we had reached our decision. I pored over the wording of every one of the messages, trying to get the right balance between being honest but not so honest that nobody would come back to work the next morning.

The last few months had taught me many things, including the need to share the good, the bad, and the ugly. But I still believed in the business and the incredible people within it, and I wanted that optimism to stay alive. Nevertheless, it was clear I needed to make fundamental changes to the way the business operated and the way I was running it.

Following so soon after the announcement about our intention to become an 'unregulated' law firm, I was nervous that everyone would become jittery. Worried for their futures, I didn't blame them, although this time, with the figures to back up what we'd done, I felt confident about the future no matter what black economic abyss we faced.

A flurry of resignations appeared in my inbox over the following weeks. Mostly, they were from other support staff, although the odd lawyer also decided it was time to move on. The messages weren't a surprise and, for the most part, were kind and understanding. Then, a couple of resignations arrived that I hadn't anticipated. Ed and Jess wrote to give notice. With my legs turning to jelly, it was lucky I was seated as the tsunami of devastation and disappointment in equal measures flowed over me.

From the moment Mairead, our new Head of Finance, started work in January, it was clear just how much we needed her and that she was the right person for the job. Nevertheless, the end of our financial year was still an uncomfortable rollercoaster of a ride.

We had to make difficult decisions, have difficult conversations, and – for me in particular – do some difficult self-reflection. I had to understand what had gone wrong in order to put it right. Yes, I had people around me advising me, and yes, I took their advice on board and made some decisions based on it. And whilst I could have pointed the finger at some of the bad advice I received, I didn't. I knew that the bottom line was *it all started and ended with me*.

Looking at the firm's history to date, I could see that no matter what I thought, I had largely run the business on intuition rather than hard data. We hadn't had the necessary systems in place to make measured decisions, and I'd allowed Stephenson Law to grow far too quickly. While additional staff hadn't been employed merely on a whim, I had agreed to take on employees without knowing for certain we could afford them.

That only changed in January 2023 when Iouri's invaluable platform enabled us to access key data in real time. Since then, I have been able to see all financial data on where the company stands at my fingertips. I can look at how much revenue we brought in last year, last month, last week or yesterday. Equally, I can see how much we spent in the same periods and on what. This allows me a measure of financial security in constantly being alert to our gross profit margin. If there are areas of concern, I am able to react accordingly, and at the same time, I can appreciate where things are going well.

It was only once I had such accurate figures that I could see how our subscription services were the part of our business that consistently performed best throughout the whole of the year, and needed to be foremost in future plans. Also, to primarily operate as an unregulated legal services provider, we would need to rethink the configuration of the entire company.

After a dreadful 12 months, as we entered a new financial year in 2023, I was once again optimistic. We were a brilliant team of around 20 rather than 40, one that was focused and heading in the same direction. In a few short months, I'd discovered that it's relatively easy to run a business when everything's going right. It's only when things start to go wrong that you really figure out who's on your side. And those are the people you need to cherish with every bone in your body.

Stephenson Law may have veered off course for a while, but now had a clear strategy and bright horizon on a different route.

PART FOUR – EXPECTATIONS

15. A New Fledgling

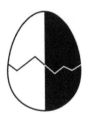

With the benefit of hindsight, I have been able to re-assess my 'annus horribilis' and realise what a seminal time it was for Stephenson Law. While that crisis period was awful to live through on a personal level – as the owner of what I now realise was a company growing too quickly to be sustainable – it was invaluable in many ways.

First up was the initial wake-up call and becoming aware of Stephenson Law's true financial situation; its profit and loss forecast and balance sheet, along with the figures surrounding its daily cash flow. What became immediately obvious was my error of judgment in thinking I was on top of everything and that the business was in a healthy financial position.

Until then, as long as there was enough money in the bank to pay the bills, I thought everything was fine. I was far more interested in developing novel methods of delivering a great service to our clients than delving into the minutiae of whether our finances were stacking up. Totally oblivious to the fact that a big increase in our annual professional indemnity insurance premium could have closed the business, my focus remained elsewhere. I'd mistakenly assumed our early pathway to success was continuing to flourish, and didn't need too much intervention or oversight to ensure it was heading in the right direction. Or at the right speed.

Secondly, the financial uncertainty meant I had to reconsider every member of staff's role within the firm. Again, before I became conscious of the circumstances surrounding our finances, I was delighted to have built such a cohesive crew: a group of people with a broad spectrum of skills that I loved having on board. Apart from during the early days of Stephenson Law – when I had far too much work to deal with personally, and knew exactly what I needed from the first lawyers I employed – many of those I'd hired since were experts in fields where I had limited experience.

I was drawn to potential employees whose applications showed a degree of individuality and who embraced our alternative approach rather than how much they could earn for the company. When assessing candidates for any position, I placed a lot of emphasis on ensuring they understood and supported the company's ethos, as well as being confident about working remotely using a variety of digital methods for communication. Consequently, we had a wonderfully diverse cohort of people who worked well together.

When the time came for me to assess their commercial value to the company, however, it was distressing to acknowledge that a few (through no fault of their own) should never have been taken on in the first place. We simply didn't have enough demand for their particular area of expertise. Some of them recognised this fact and were understanding when I had to make them redundant. For me, making someone redundant could never be a decision taken lightly. It was so painful to both acknowledge the need and execute the deed that I knew I'd do everything necessary to avoid ever finding myself in that position again.

Another painful lesson was the discovery that no matter how much I liked to spend time with members of staff and took pleasure in their company, I was still their boss. While we may have enjoyed a coffee or a meal together and appreciated one another's sense of humour, sense of dress or tattoos, we always remained employer and employee. We weren't mates. We could not have an equal relationship.

'That's not always the case,' someone said when I mentioned this during a recent reunion of students from my time at Bath University. 'I work in a small company with a great atmosphere – I was even invited to the owner's wedding. We're definitely friends.'

'I like to think we're much more than colleagues,' another person added. 'I may be the boss on paper, but we spend so much time together, with mutual respect and support for one another, that I do believe friendships develop.'

Until things went awry at Stephenson Law, I would have held similar beliefs to both of these people. However, when you get down to the nitty-gritty, it's obvious that the relationship between employer and employee can never be that of friends where there is an implicit understanding of equality. The basic tenet of employment in a capitalist organisation is for one person to make money out of someone else's endeavour. It's not just buying someone's time; it's buying someone's time to make money out of it.

I now accept that I can like, admire and respect the people I employ, but they can only become friends when I no longer pay them to work for me.

The final and probably the most important outcome in the fallout from my annus horribilis was the creation of Springbird IP. This separate company, previously a part of Stephenson Law, came into being as a result of the necessary restructuring of the firm.

When I investigated the pros and cons of remaining a regulated law firm, it involved considering the long-term implications of such a decision on each sector of the company. By design, all departments worked closely together and often shared clients through work emanating from one of our subscription services or putting together tailor-made packages for specific customers. While the system operated smoothly, with the various areas of expertise integrating seamlessly on the whole, there was one exception: our trade mark team. It was a thriving department that was brilliantly managed but very much on its own trajectory. As well as using different systems and pricing models from the rest of Stephenson Law, it also attracted a different type of client. While much appreciated and respected, our very own IP department was effectively the cuckoo in our flamingo's nest!

Before the insurance fiasco of June 2022, or our downturn of business due to the exponential rise in both interest and inflation rates, the IP team was already on a different pathway from the rest of the company. It was as if I was the CEO running two different businesses under one hypothetical roof. So, while deliberating on which way to go forward, I wondered if this was the time to make it official and create a separate business: Springbird IP. Instead of being our flamingo's 'cuckoo', it would be its fledgling, so to speak, and always remain part of our flock. Upholding our ethos and values, we would help it become established as a standalone powerhouse of IP expertise. I would retain a small financial interest while allowing Springbird the freedom to go in the direction most suited to its needs. I also knew that it would be headed by the most committed and accomplished chartered trade mark attorney, Laura West.

When she joined us back in 2021, it was apparent that Laura shared my appetite for overhauling the legal industry. This made her the perfect new Head of IP, and aware of her ambition within her chosen area of law, she was very much part of my future plans for the division that would eventually become Springbird IP. She had witnessed the inefficiencies of the trade mark world, the pain points of her clients, and the failures of the industry to deliver expertise in a way that was efficient in addressing modern demands. In traditional IP firms, where attorneys – keen to reach their monthly billable hour targets – can be reticent to share projects with colleagues, clients can suffer delays in receiving appropriate advice. This may happen if their attorney is on holiday or unwell and can be devastating for a young firm if a time-critical issue arises, as described below with the travel wellness company, 15th Degree.

Laura was an immediate asset to Stephenson Law and contributed greatly to the success of our subscription models. As I became more certain that the IP division would benefit from having more independence, I felt confident that Laura was the person to lead it, that she would be keen to add her own flavour and texture in creating a similar model to that of Stephenson Law.

'Have you ever thought of running your own company?' I asked her. It was a virtual meeting, and seeing her eyes widen with the hint of a smile before she responded, I already knew the answer.

'If I did,' she replied. 'It would be on similar lines to Stephenson Law – I'm sure that's the way forward.'

This was music to my ears and we soon came to an agreement. Like me, Laura was confident that by fixing costs, reducing admin, and bundling services for the benefit of clients, the new fledgling would have a great life ahead. An expert in her field, Laura has been recognised by the Legal 500 (one of the world's most prestigious legal publications, providing the largest and most comprehensive survey of the global legal market) as an 'Exceptionally efficient and responsive trade mark attorney.' She is also acknowledged in the World IP Review Leaders Directory 2022 as a global IP leader.

Springbird IP was born out of a belief that intellectual property protection needs to match the vigour of today's brands. With the worldwide reach of digital information easily accessible to anyone with a smartphone, when new products are developed, it doesn't take long for others to attempt to copy or clone them. For IP firms to flourish in this global marketplace, they have to react accordingly with rapid responses and appropriate solutions. 'Having previously worked with large, corporate IP attorneys who didn't understand the fragile nature of early business, being introduced to Springbird answered all my IP prayers,' said Papillon Luck, the founder of 15th Degree. 'They helped me navigate sending a cease and desist letter to a brand infringing on our marks, during the process of selling marks to another global company. What could have become complicated and expensive was handled with care, speed, efficiency and attention to detail... but what's just as important as their extensive IP knowledge, is that they are all really fun to work with. If Springbird can make trademarks fun, you know you've got the right team supporting you!'

15th Degree, like many modern startups, is targeting a market that didn't exist 20 years ago. As a 'travel wellness company', it has developed JetFuel, a range of food supplements aimed at reducing tiredness and fatigue in frequent flyers. Although the word 'wellness' was first coined in the late 1950s, it was a very niche area until exploding into everyone's consciousness over the last decade or so. Since then, as well as individuals becoming more aware of their general sense of 'wellbeing', it is increasingly common for large employers to have 'workplace wellness schemes'. Given the evidence that for every dollar spent on such programmes, around five dollars is saved in medical expenses and absenteeism, these policies continue to expand exponentially.[36] After a career in international banking and hedge funds, Papillon Luck was discerning in her choice of starting a business in a growing industry, and chose an appropriately forward-thinking IP provider.

As to be expected in a specialist organisation, Springbird dives deep into IP matters, from intellectual property strategy to civil recovery to IP enforcement. But perhaps the most exciting thing about the brand is its intellectual property subscription, which delivers *end-to-end* trade mark and design portfolio support.

While the industry as a whole is replete with legal talent, it's also burdened by clock-watching, unpredictable fees, and mountains of admin. Intellectual property protection is phenomenally important to any business with a brand it values. And yet, to protect that brand and what it stands for

---

[36] Forbes, 11th June 2019

can be a protracted and complicated legal process that is both expensive and never-ending. From the moment Laura first joined Stephenson Law, she knew she could build a team that offered a better and more streamlined level of service than was expected within the industry.

Today, Springbird IP's focus is on brands with vast and bespoke IP needs rather than the everyday. Its services are delivered by people who share the Stephenson Law ethos of openness and transparency. It has created a pioneering 'Infinitely Springbird' subscription that allows clients to budget with clarity and protect IP with confidence. It put an end to the processing of a gamut of IP-focused invoices – such as one for a cease and desist letter, or one for renewing a trade mark. Instead, there is one fixed annual fee based on the number of trade marks or designs to be protected, that covers searches, filing, applications, renewals, watching services and prosecution. It provides thorough IP audits, due diligence and forward-thinking strategy to ensure clients can truly strengthen and maximise their brand while knowing how much its 'legals' will cost.

Already boasting big-name consumer brands, such as Gymshark, Butternut Box, Huel, and Fever-Tree, Springbird IP is trusted to protect some of the most valuable intellectual property portfolios in the world. I am inordinately proud to have been involved in its establishment and convinced it has a great future with Laura as its CEO.

Once the decision had been taken for Springbird IP to be set up as a separate business, restructuring Stephenson Law became less complicated. It would also become an unregulated law firm while helping Springbird IP leave our corporate nest. I would only remain the CEO of Stephenson

Law, where I would continue to challenge the legal industry's norms and vigorously promote our subscription services.

While this sounds quite straightforward, once a law firm has chosen to be regulated by the SRA, there is no way for it to become deregulated. Instead, it has to cease trading. Then, depending on its level of turnover, a sum of money will be paid to its insurer in case a client should choose to sue at some future date. I discovered that if Stephenson Law – with a turnover of around £3.5m at this time – chose to cease trading, our insurers could reasonably ask us for a sum in the region of £600,000 to be paid to them to cover potential costs as a 'run off' insurance premium.

This was obviously not a realistic proposition, given our dire financial straits. Instead, and like other law firms wishing to 'deregulate', we set up a new company into which we transferred the vast majority of our business and all subscription and employment contracts. The original regulated Stephenson Law business would continue to trade, albeit with a very low turnover, until such time as its 'run off' insurance levy became affordable.

Despite the issues I had to deal with when investigating how Stephenson Law could operate as an unregulated law firm in 2022, given the choices available to me back in 2017 and the criteria by which I made my decision to become a regulated law firm, I still think I made the right choice. However, when I revisited the options available today, I discovered changes to what had previously been available.

Since 2019, solicitors have been allowed to deliver 'non-reserved' legal services to the public from a business not regulated by the SRA. This development was important for my new company, given that every service Stephenson Law delivered fell into the 'non-reserved' category. It meant we could readily carry on our work as before without the caveat of having onerous levels of professional indemnity insurance, whilst enabling my lawyers to retain their practising certificates. At the same time, not having the SRA looming over us meant we could be much more agile and ready to change our delivery methods if that suited our clients' needs. This was of specific importance given the rapidly changing world of technology, a sector with which we were particularly involved. If we wanted to revise the manner in which we provided our data protection or employment law advice, we wouldn't have to ask ourselves, 'Will this be SRA compliant?' Also, should we choose at some future date to bring in a co-owner or a new director, those individuals would no longer need SRA approval prior to appointment.

An integral part of the Stephenson Law ethos was creating and maintaining a good rapport with clients on a human level to ensure that what we provided was appropriate and mutually beneficial. As a result, we were completely open about the planned changes and the reasoning behind them. With many of our clients being early-stage companies, such as our own, they were both encouraging and appreciative of what we aimed to achieve. They could also see the advantages we would have in being more flexible in our service delivery without having to constantly refer to SRA compliance. When it came to the staff, it was more than heart-warming to register the positive response when I explained the new company setup. Everyone was supportive and understood how it made sense for Springbird IP to become independent while Stephenson Law concentrated on its own future.

No longer having to consider the particularities of how the IP team operated, I was able to further streamline our services to focus on our subscriptions. Each of our subscriptions has been designed to fit the needs of our clients rather than us creating a singular product to then promote, market, and sell. We haven't had to persuade or even demonstrate how suitable they are to our clients' wants because they're effectively tailor-made. I believe this concept of exploring the needs of clients and then building a service to accommodate those necessities explains the growing popularity of our subscription models.

Given the above, I can now state with confidence that – since early 2023 – we are far stronger than before and as much in control of our destiny as we can be. I don't underestimate how fragile we were back in mid-2022, and considering the catastrophic demise of some major banks in earlier periods of recession, I would be foolish to suggest there won't be stormy times ahead. Nevertheless, since the restructuring, we have been steadily progressing to carefully grow our subscription services in the knowledge that they are bound to vary according to future demand.

On a personal level, it was a massive relief to discover that we hadn't lost any clients or members of staff when all the changes had been put in place. It was an affirmation that we'd done what needed to be done for the good of everyone. All the same, it had been a fraught and stressful time during which I knew I'd demanded too much of my amazing husband, Pete.

Lydia was largely making her way in the world, and although there were regular trips to our Amsterdam home, she was a young adult following her own passions. However, our two young sons, Adam and Bertie, still needed lots of parental input, and as their Easter holidays approached, I couldn't wait to spend some time with them.

'Are you coming, too?' Adam asked me incredulously when we were preparing a picnic for what would be a very windy trip to a local beach one Sunday morning. Much as we love living in Amsterdam, the weather is no more predictable or sunny than in the UK, and ever since we first moved here, Pete likes to make the most of any clear blue sky on a weekend! For quite a long time, I'd been far too occupied with work to join my boys on all their adventures. And I'm ashamed to admit that sometimes – when Adam and Bertie returned home excitedly to tell me what they'd been up to – I was too tired to pay much attention.

'I certainly am,' I replied as I pulled my son in for a hug and felt his silky hair on my cheek. Fully aware of how quickly he was growing up, it was good to know that Stephenson Law was back on track, and I could once again prioritise my children's wellbeing rather than that of my company.

As we entered a new financial year in April 2023, it felt very much like a new beginning. Unlike 2017, I had the security of a brilliant team of experts working alongside me and a broad cohort of clients with whom we had built strong relationships. It was difficult to fully comprehend just how much I'd learned over the previous six years and I knew – going forward – that there would be much more to learn. However, there could be no argument that, despite the various traumas experienced, I had founded a successful law firm that offered a brilliant service to its clients in a very different manner to the old traditional legal partnerships. Indeed, both Stephenson Law and Springbird IP were on a mission to revolutionise legal services for the better, and would continue to chart new waters fearlessly.

16. Still Learning

I continue to advocate that the legal industry must embrace change for it to flourish, and promote Stephenson Law's success as evidence. Given its unusual business model, I'm frequently asked to comment on its achievements and offer advice to younger lawyers starting out on what they hope to be successful careers. As a result, I've pondered how success can or should be defined.

Is success a corner office overlooking the city? A wallet filled with cash? A career littered with accolades and awards? Increasingly senior titles in a long-established firm? Is it more personal than material gain, and what can be measured from the outside? Or should success be about achieving a sense of fulfilment for oneself more than anything else?

When it comes to professional achievement in the legal field, it has generally been accepted that the route is well-trodden and 'mapped out' for any ambitious youngster wanting to pursue it. They need to get good grades, have a leg up into the right firms, work hard and then scramble up towards making partner. However, the way to the top isn't always as straightforward or simple as it might seem, and one person's triumph may not be described as such by another. While great exam results, a strong CV and a killer work ethic will work for some, those attributes won't guarantee success for everyone. And nor will they be necessary for others. How do I know? Because when it came to my own experience of how to succeed, I had to beat my own path. One that was filled with hidden twists and turns that weren't always easy to overcome.

Today, I'm the CEO of a multi-award-winning legal services firm. However, at the beginning of my career, I was a single mother clambering for a sense of stability. Years were spent simply learning how to survive and doing what I could to keep my head above water. I didn't get record-busting grades. I didn't begin my career in a City firm. And the road to what I would describe as success was far from straightforward. While other lawyers of my age were stepping onto each rung of the long-established legal career ladder, I was beginning to realise it wasn't going to happen for me. The primary ingredients for what I wanted to achieve were far more complex than exam results or knowing the right people.

I began to understand how, as an individual in an aggressively demanding industry, there would always be others with better qualifications, more influence, and more expertise than me. However, while there may be people with whom I couldn't compete in a technical capacity, it was unlikely that they would also display my combined levels of drive, persistence, and sheer determination.

Something unique about every one of us is our ability to manage the highs, cope with the lows, and maintain tenacity when the going gets tough. If there's one thing I've understood and experienced intimately as an adult woman, it's that when it comes to life, there is only one guarantee: it's unpredictable. I now believe that my resilience in dealing with difficult circumstances – some as a result of my own misjudgements and others not – has been my greatest asset.

So, how did I build my resilience? How did I pivot from being a struggling teenage mother to heading up a law firm? What helped me go the distance and not give in along the way?

These aren't easy questions to answer, but after consideration, I believe the following eight factors have been key.

1. Embrace Emotional Intelligence

There are quite a few useful things that schools and colleges neglect to teach their students. Practical things like how to complete a tax return, change a tyre, or boil an egg, as well as other, less tangible things such as how to cope with difficult situations and value different perspectives. And yet, nurturing an understanding of emotional intelligence is one of the secrets to an easier life and career. It's a broad term that encompasses managing awkward conversations with others, alongside recognising our own unconscious biases, reactions and fears. We are all complex human beings, and our interactions with each other are fundamental to both our personal and professional lives.

Early in my adult life as a young parent, I subsisted on patchy sleep and a shoestring budget where every endeavour to improve things was a struggle. It's fair to say that when it came to finding the time to study – so that I could make our lives better – I often felt I was running on empty. If I had let this weariness overcome me, my ability to cope with what had to be done would have become even more affected. Instead, by confronting my feelings of frustration and *accepting* them, I was able to take each day at a time. Slowly, I began to recognise I was making progress and that each period of study was taking me forward. I now know that the importance of being able to confront and own feelings extends to the wider professional world. And this includes the legal world.

Law is a service industry that deals with one group of people who deliver a service to another group of people. Both groups comprise individuals who have unique perspectives on what to expect from that service. As a business that evolves around people's expectations, those of us who can develop the 'soft skills' required to ensure these are acknowledged and understood gain an advantage. Limitless complications will arise over the course of a career that deals with human beings, and knowing how to approach those situations with empathy and patience is a priceless skill.

2. Stop the Negative Self-Talk

When discussing unconscious bias in an earlier chapter, I mentioned that women are as guilty as men for having unreasonable expectations of other women. They are often quick to find fault in new mothers, whether it's those who go back to work too soon after giving birth or those who choose to be stay-at-home parents. Either way, new mums are being criticised by the very people who should be supporting them.

That same unconscious bias is at play within each of us when we find reasons to blame ourselves when things go wrong. There are lots of ways we self-sabotage, from simply telling ourselves we're not good enough to do the job, or by taking responsibility for problems that were completely out of our control.

As a business owner, I make dozens of decisions a day, and when some of those inevitably transpire to be mistakes, I often beat myself up for getting it wrong.

So often, we're our own worst critics, but that negative self-talk is really dangerous. It creates our reality; if we tell ourselves we're not good enough, eventually we truly believe it. And if we don't believe in ourselves, how can we expect anyone else to?

I work hard every day to identify any negative self-talk and stop it. I'm not perfect at it, but the more I practise, the better I get. Some days, I feel stronger than others and recognise that it's important to treat myself with the love and respect I try to offer others.

3. Recognise the Mask and Shell

I remember a time when I'd look at others of a similar age or a similar time of life to me and think they had everything figured out while I was struggling. They always looked like they'd just stepped out of the shower and into newly pressed clothes. They had a healthy glow with just the right amount of make-up, manicured nails and a perfect haircut. Their car was immaculate inside and out despite being used for the daily school run. Their children seemed to be real-life angels, and their homes were as tidy as those in glossy magazines.

It took a while for me to understand that people show the world what they want other people to see. That's not a criticism, and it's what we all do to a certain degree. We choose to present the version of ourselves that we're most comfortable sharing. It's a mask that we hope others – particularly our peers – will find attractive, as well as a carapace behind which we can hide and protect ourselves. In the same way as the blurb and design of a book jacket can only offer a glimpse of what the reader will discover inside, the clothes we wear and the colour of our hair only offer a limited perspective of the very complex person they cover.

4. Create Clear Goals

I wrote earlier about the value of a business plan when setting up a new company. Having a clear vision of what I wanted to achieve with Stephenson Law was important from the very beginning. It's only by having aims and realistic objectives that a viable pathway to reach them can be created.

As a younger woman, I found it difficult to articulate what I wanted to accomplish, but I've now grown into a seriously goal-driven person. I spend time thinking about my goals, discussing them with those closest to me, writing them down and monitoring them. I have personal goals, shared goals with Pete, and business goals.

It might sound eccentric or even cheesy, but I also believe in the power of visualisation. I'm convinced that because I was always able to visualise myself, my life, and my business in the future, I was able to take steps towards that vision. I continue to do so, and with a clear visualisation, I feel confident I will reach my goals.

5. Build Self-Discipline

How easy is it to reach for a chocolate bar instead of an apple? Or find an excuse not to go for a run today? Or buy those expensive designer sunglasses knowing they're not affordable and could easily be lost?

It takes immense self-discipline to choose long-term success over instant gratification. We all want to feel good now. So why not worry about how we feel in the future when we get there?

Because we regret those impulsive decisions we made yesterday and know we made bad choices that will hold us back, my advice is to create good routines that will grow into good habits. Self-awareness is important when designing the routine to ensure it suits our personality. For myself, I always exercise first thing in the morning because I know I'll find an excuse later in the day and be far too busy to find the time again. I also know that as soon as I see junk food, I eat it! As a result, I insist that chocolate and other unhealthy goodies are kept out of sight.

It takes time to build good habits, but – as boring as it sounds –they work!

6. Set Boundaries

One of the hardest words for me to say is 'No'. Yet this is something I have learned is imperative in attempting to juggle motherhood and my career. Especially when saying 'Yes' seems to be the easiest option despite it not being the correct one.

As a lawyer and entrepreneur who wants my business to flourish, I've always found it difficult to turn down opportunities, even when they may be tough to achieve. I'm in the business of making things happen, and as someone driven to deliver the best each and every time, it can feel incredibly counterproductive to put on the brakes. While law school and my legal training taught me to cope with the endless demands of the legal world, it was parenthood that taught me how important it is sometimes to say 'No'.

Along with countless others, I would love to be everything to everyone, and while Stephenson Law is part of who I am, there is no greater priority for me than being a parent.

Despite being blessed with a remarkably supportive husband who is a wonderful father to my three children, I too have a role in their lives. And I discovered that for me to give my best as a CEO, as well as a mother, I had to invest in myself.

That meant understanding my boundaries and confronting my fears. I needed to recognise when I could readily deal with the dual demands of life at home or work, and when it was time for me to refuel. If I found my mind wandering when one of my boys was telling me about his day, or that I had to read a work document several times before the information sunk in, I knew I was doing too much. This realisation gave me permission for time out, the space to grow and, in my opinion, become a better, more reasoned version of myself.

This isn't to say that I no longer make mistakes and say 'Yes' when I should say 'No' or vice versa. Nevertheless, even when things were at their worst in my professional life, although I may have missed many a family weekend trip, our evening meals were always family meals; and I always saw my boys off to school each morning. Being a parent is challenging, as is running a business; both are equally rewarding in return.

Knowing my limits and understanding them has generally allowed me to continue juggling my two different lives.

7. Self-Awareness

Many of us lead full and hectic lives where every waking moment is accounted for. Days go by without consideration for our emotional well-being and freedom of thought. Sometimes, we are so busy that we don't notice others entering our lives who can have a negative influence on our self-perception. I would describe such people as toxic, and they can be difficult to identify, having always appeared to have our best interests at heart. Smooth talkers who are only too ready to flatter; they are disarmingly friendly and ready to advise. As a result, it can be easy to internalise their prejudices or unreasonable expectations and adopt them as if they were our own. These individuals may be business colleagues, friends, members of our family or perhaps professional 'influencers' – people we follow online and have admired and listened to from afar.

It is tough to always look objectively at how we judge ourselves and others, whether we are making assessments based on our own experiences and beliefs or someone else's. However, if we do identify someone who has an adverse influence on our lives, we need to deal with them. If direct confrontation isn't a practical option, setting boundaries on what future role they will play may be effective, and if that doesn't work, they may need to be avoided completely.

For those of us who work hard to live a good and reasonable life where we treat others with love and compassion, we should remember that we too are valuable. We deserve to be surrounded by people that love and support us unconditionally. Nobody should settle for anything less than that.

8. Never Stop Learning

Stephenson Law wasn't my first business, nor was the legal industry my first choice of career. As previously mentioned, my first business failed to make any money, and my first career in HR failed to make me happy. I learned from both experiences and moved on to train as a lawyer. Once qualified, I bounced from firm to firm in search of somewhere to settle and enjoy a fulfilling professional life. It didn't take long for me to learn that while I'd found a fascinating industry, I couldn't find a suitable company within which to build a suitable career. Instead, a decade after beginning my legal training, by founding my own firm I found my professional home and had learned I had strengths that went beyond the traditional lawyer's career path.

I was a seasoned professional in 'constantly learning', a skill that would see me overcome countless obstacles and always look to better my understanding of the world around me.

Ever since gaining my first degree from the University of Bath in 2005, I've never spent more than a year away from studying for further qualifications. After qualifying as a solicitor, I went on to obtain other postgraduate legal diplomas through different British universities. On moving to the Netherlands and wanting to extend my breadth of entrepreneurial expertise, I took on the demands of an Executive MBA at the University of Amsterdam.

As a diligent student, I like to learn in a formal manner with an advanced agenda and specific goal to attain. Others prefer a more relaxed approach. Either way, when talking to anyone with the ambition to progress further in their career, ongoing learning opportunities or 'professional development' is always a major part of career progression.

Recognising there is always more to learn is probably the most important of the eight factors behind the success I've achieved to date. Indeed, I can't imagine ever reaching the point where I don't feel there's more I need to learn. There's still so much to look forward to with Stephenson Law, and beyond that, I'm sure my learning days are far from over.

17. Taking My Vision Forward

In 2017, just a few months after the birth of my third child, I started Stephenson Law. I had Pete by my side to make sure everything ran smoothly on the home front and just £2,000 in the bank.

After spending £300 on branding, £400 on a website and arranging finance to cover professional indemnity insurance, the remainder of my budget went to the legal regulator, the SRA. I then went out to find and win clients.

With a £17k turnover in my first month, I can remember the sense of relief like it was yesterday. It meant that my dream of creating a different kind of law firm might actually be achievable. Of course, it wasn't long before I began to panic about where the work would come from. With nowhere to go for advice, or anyone to ask other than the naysayers who said I would never succeed, I felt very alone. That's when I realised what it feels like to be the founder of a company, and despite the countless periods of panic I've experienced since, my decision to establish Stephenson Law was a good one. My dream has come true and is part of a definitive and important moment in British legal history. For the first time, law firms like mine – firms that are designed for the needs of today's diverse and multicultural world – not only exist but are growing by the day and flourishing across the industry.

My route to becoming a solicitor wasn't straightforward. Even before qualifying, I was starting to realise that while I'd chosen an interesting and rewarding career path, it wasn't one that welcomed people like me. People who didn't fit the traditional concept of what a lawyer should look and behave like. I was a woman and mother covered in tattoos who had ideas and opinions. This seemed to bother my bosses more than whether or not I was an excellent lawyer. It was soon clear that I'd entered an archaic profession with such outdated values and methodologies that it would never appreciate what I (or others like me) could offer.

Although I was largely unaware of it, around the time I was considering how to start Stephenson Law, there were already some relatively new legal firms that had chosen a different model to that of the pyramid-shaped, hierarchical, traditional legal partnership. They, too, were seeking change and taking unorthodox decisions to succeed. Today, there are big and small legal firms that have recognised the world is changing, and the legal industry as a whole needs to change with it.

According to statistics from the SRA, the proportion of legal establishments operating under a traditional partnership model more than halved in the decade to 2021 from a third to just 14%. During the same period, the proportion of solicitors' firms run as limited companies shot up from 20% to 50%.

It was the Legal Services Act of 2007 that ushered in the possibility of alternative business structures to own and manage firms rather than lawyers. By choosing to set up limited companies rather than limited partnerships, these new business structures have been enabled to bring in fresh and more reliable opportunities for long-term investment. They don't have to rely on the whims of senior partners to decide whether or not to update the company's IT system despite it being 15 years old. They are run by corporate professionals rather than grey-haired lawyers who, while they may have climbed to the tops of their careers, are not businessmen and can barely manage a conference call on their mobile phones. The modern CEO has to satisfy the demands of the company's shareholders and investors rather than solicitors who are counting down the days to retirement. These modern legal structures have been concentrating on the long game, and over the past decade, some have grown into global giants with diverse business interests. Equally, the legal sector has become noticed by international accountancy firms and business consultants such as EY, KPMG and PWC, who have broadened their areas of interest accordingly.

Another new business model that has become increasingly common is that of the 'dispersed' firm. This essentially provides a platform for solicitors who wish to practice law independently but don't want to run a law firm. It's similar in design to that of barristers' chambers, where the secretarial, administrative, marketing and insurance functions are undertaken on behalf of the solicitor. The lawyers who choose this method often want the freedom to choose their client lists, work from home, and operate the hours that suit them in order for their professional lives to fit in comfortably with their private lives. Equally, they may have the flexibility to accommodate clients who want them to work in-house and support an existing legal team.

Dispersed firms allow lawyers to be themselves. They offer careers to those of us who do not fit the mould of the conventional besuited solicitor with far more choice and autonomy than is available in a traditional law firm. Before creating Stephenson Law, I worked successfully in a freelance capacity for several years. I enjoyed the freedom and knew the quality of my work assured a secure future, but it didn't fulfil my desire to challenge the system. I wanted to work under a different, fairer and more transparent system.

This was how I came to the conclusion that if I wanted to build a fulfilling career in law, I would have to start a firm with my *own values*. One that recognises difference can be an advantage.

After taking the leap and founding Stephenson Law, the existence of social media was vital to its growth. This modern method of digital communication was how I made contact with potential clients and (eventually) persuaded people to come and work with me. And it was by posting my opinions about the state of the British legal industry on LinkedIn that I came across other young challenger law firms. I discovered I wasn't the only legal maverick trying to establish myself in the industry; there were other lawyer-entrepreneurs like me who wanted fundamental change. Others who, against the odds, had started their own firms for a wide variety of reasons and in just as many ways. I no longer felt so alone in trying to set up an alternative to the traditional partnership model but part of a tribe that was dispirited with the status quo and challenged its authority.

As we got to know one another and discussed our ideas about building brands and delivering legal services, I could see that we had a lot in common. While our backgrounds, legal areas and methods of delivery were more varied than a box of Liquorice Allsorts, our basic beliefs about the necessity for the legal industry to reflect the needs and populations of today's world were the same. As a result of this, I decided to create an online membership community of like-minded law firm leaders, and Lawscape was born.

We are a disparate group that are passionate about our work, and having often started as a single lawyer, frequently offer legal services in niche areas rather than across the board. Some are exploring alternative pricing models and have gone along the route of off-the-shelf legal packages; others have specialised in specific services for specific industries such as real estate, education or health. We even have a tree specialist!

For Stephenson Law, with our market being predominantly scale-ups in the tech industry, a model based on legal subscriptions has proved to be popular as well as sustainable and is what we are taking forward. It gives clients the security of knowing how much their legal costs will be over a given period of time, which I know is important for young businesses. From our perspective, the subscription model allows us the financial security to invest in the best lawyers and technology to ensure a service second to none. And while we are certainly not the only legal company offering subscription packages to our clients, I believe we are unique at this time in offering such a broad, multi-disciplinary service.

As mentioned above, when I founded Stephenson Law, there was nowhere and no one to turn to for advice. I was prepared for the challenge, ready for innovation, and willing to work very hard. However, I wasn't prepared for just how lonely it is being the person at the top. Not only was it difficult to access information to help build my business, it was also tough not being able to discuss the daily problems I faced with others going through similar issues.

Through Lawscape, this is no longer the case. It has brought together some of the brightest, most innovative and diverse leaders working in the industry. We are there to support one another and help nurture those starting out afresh so that – collectively – we can create a legal industry fit for the 21st century. Along with others, I've done my very best to share the experiences, good and bad, of what it's been like to build a successful law firm. As a leader for change, I want to curate the perfect community in which we can learn from each other and grow our firms to the next level.

While specifically aimed at legal firms, people join Lawscape from backgrounds in management, finance and marketing, as well as law. It is a peer-to-peer network supporting the future of modern law firms as well as encouraging others who wish to establish their own law firms. Through trial and error, it took me six years to build a business that's on steady ground, and other firms have taken longer. I also know of owners who suffered far more than me on both professional and personal levels while pursuing their dream to challenge the industry and create a better type of law firm.

Through Lawscape, we're hoping to help new legal start-ups avoid some of our mistakes by offering monthly 'clinics' and a variety of masterclasses hosted by outside experts providing training in pretty much any area where a young law firm may need assistance – whether designing a long-term strategy, sales and pricing, hiring and managing a team, marketing and building a brand or tech, and innovation.

Lawscape is just one example of current progress in the legal world and while it may not be moving forward rapidly, there is nevertheless tangible change afoot. After all, almost every City law firm proudly proclaims an outreach programme to attract under-represented sectors of the population and offer paid paternity leave… even if it's not encouraged. While I'm sure there are some who genuinely want change, I remain sceptical about how effective such programmes will prove to be in the short to medium term. It is attitudes more than rules that need to change, and there are few who would argue that the vast majority of law firms today remain steeped in tradition, archaic practices and outdated perspectives.

Nevertheless, they can't avoid the widespread evidence that the most successful businesses in the FTSE 100 and Dow Jones are usually those with the most diverse boardrooms. Nor can they avoid the commercial interest some of these big global corporations have in the British legal sector. I'm hopeful that this could be the trigger to finally change attitudes and acknowledge that innovation is essential for the future success of the industry. In the long term, I believe this is the only way the industry will be able to attract and keep diverse, talented and creative new lawyers.

Within my own legal sphere, I'm sure there are more exciting times ahead for Stephenson Law, Springbird IP, and all the other challenger legal firms that are growing by the day. Along with the rest of the Lawscape community, I will doubtlessly encounter further barriers that need to be broken down and boundaries I will refuse to recognise.

Have I got all the answers to enable some sort of legal Nirvana? Of course not. But as an outlaw – 'one that is unconventional or rebellious' – I'm on a mission to help bring about positive change to a profession in desperate need for it. One that, in some form or another, we all rely on. And I will continue to do so until such time that a traditional law firm reflects the community it serves with a provision of legal expertise appropriately valued and delivered without prejudice.

Epilogue

October
2023

Stephenson Law built its reputation in the legal industry by ruffling feathers, earning its place by growing a flock of like-minded lawyers and securing its impact by helping fast-growth scaleups in the UK to soar.

When, early in 2023, we took the decision to operate as an unregulated legal services provider, we wanted to rebrand the firm in a manner synonymous with our history of defying the status quo. Rather than simply update our trade mark or our mantra 'be a flamingo in a flock of pigeons', we chose to change our name to 'Plume': the most noticeable feather on the grandest of birds. I am incredibly proud of what Stephenson Law has achieved, but feel it's time to move on from the ancient tradition of naming firms after founders.

Plume is ready to move forward, to continue with more colourful and innovative ways to deliver legal services.

Alice

Other Books from the Publisher

"Open and honest... entertaining and informative. A cracking read." **Magistrates' Blog**

THE SECRET MAGISTRATE

"I thoroughly recommend this book which powerfully and entertainingly addresses both the inherent strengths and the present weaknesses of the Magistrates' Court system." **Anthony Metzer QC**

Every criminal case starts in a magistrates' court, and most end there. Last year, the 14,000 magistrates of England & Wales dealt with almost 1.4 million cases. *The Secret Magistrate* takes the reader on an eye-opening, behind-the-scenes tour of a year in the life of an inner-city magistrate.

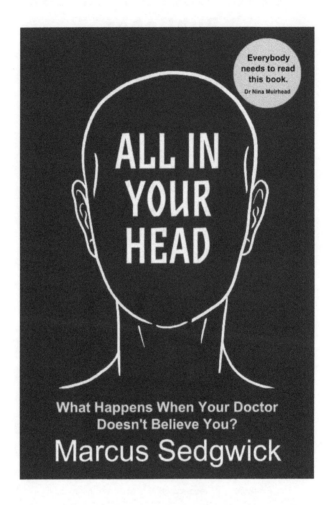

All In Your Head is about what happens when your doctor doesn't believe that you're ill. When they think you are imagining a serious ailment, or worse, faking it.

With honesty, and at times, dark humour, *All In Your Head* – from multiple award-winning author Marcus Sedgwick – explores how four simple words can make you question your sense of reality.

Nick Charles MBE is a pioneer in treating alcohol dependency. But Nick's decorated success overlays an extraordinary and unforgettable personal journey, for Nick was once an alcoholic vagrant sleeping rough on the streets of London.

Spend Green and Save The World is a practical guide on what you can do to make a difference. And the amazing thing is that it only takes 3.5% of a population to act in order to create cultural change, and a mindshift in wider thinking! By coming together and using our consumer power – as part of The Consumer-Led Movement – we can influence businesses and government policy, and rapidly shape a better future. All through consciously choosing how we spend our money.

Milton Keynes UK
Ingram Content Group UK Ltd.
UKHW040052201123
432895UK00004B/26

9 781914 066382